Patchwork

A World Tour

CATHERINE LEGRAND

Patchwork

A World Tour

PREFACE

'I would like to gather all these little pieces of mauve,
turquoise, violet, these little flowers of crimson, cinnabar,
vermilion, and sew them all by hand... I will embroider
your name, your name in couched golden thread on
the umber ground!'
Bernard-Marie Koltès, *Black Battles with Dogs* (1979)

Patchwork is a term that covers a broad variety of textile
techniques. In addition to traditional forms of pieced
work sewn together with invisible stitching, it can also
include appliqué, reverse appliqué and visible mending
methods such as *boro* stitching. Like a patchwork, this
book is made up of textiles from all over the world,
stitched together to form a whole. In place of scraps
of fabric, you'll see samples of global cultures and
traditions, perhaps a Congolese *n'tchak* alongside a *mola*
from Panama, or a Miao baby carrier next to an Amish
quilt. Like a patchwork, diversity becomes unity, variety
becomes cohesion, imagination brings the whole thing
to life and encourages us to view each piece as a whole
and the whole as more than the sum of its parts. In the
deepest sense, this book is composed from fragments
of human lives laid side by side in order to illustrate this
shared global artform, in a way that allows the creativity
and hard work of its practitioners to shine through.

Note:
When illustrations are undated,
it is reasonable to assume that
the pieces originate from the
second half of the 20th century.

INTRODUCTION

My own passion for patchwork first began at the American Folk Art Museum, a small museum located close to MoMA in New York. An exhibition of Jonathan Holstein's quilt collection, held in 1972 at the Musée des Arts Décoratifs in Paris, only intensified my interest. In 1977, I opened À La Bonne Renommée, a textile design boutique and studio in Le Marais, Paris, in collaboration with my friend and colleague Elisabeth Gratacap. Throughout this thirty-five year adventure, patchwork has played a part in each of our collections. Like a leitmotif, it reappears summer and winter, on hats, coats, bags or cushions. As the seasons go by, it may be subtle or bold, traditional or quirky, historical or international. Our creations take their inspiration from travelling, museums, paintings and books, forming an entire imaginative world. We also published a book, *À La Bonne Renommée, 136 saisons*, telling the tale of this journey.

'Patchwork is the most misleading word in the world for a way of crossing space and time using a needle and your imagination,' the journalist and author Claude Fauque wrote. Patchwork is the name for a technique and also for objects created using that technique, which could be bedlinen, tablecloths, wall hangings, clothing or a wide range of other items. The word patchwork can also be used for textiles that have nothing to do with the traditional technique except its sense of abundance. By extrapolation, the word 'patchwork' can describe any kind of mixture, jumble, confusion or miscellany, referring to architecture, music, a style of writing, people, and even ideas.

Even within the realm of textiles, the term patchwork can refer to multiple techniques. Here, it is used not just for pieces of fabric assembled with stitching on the reverse but also for appliqué, a complementary way of stitching fabric motifs to a base material. The crafts of reverse appliqué and quilting are featured too. Elements such as embroidery, beading, braid or tiny mirrors may be added, but the resulting piece can still be called patchwork.

'Part of a bed that covers it from the head to the foot and which extends down to the base. Patchworks may be made of the richest fabrics or the most simple; there are those for winter and those for summer, some light, some warm and often stitched through.' This definition of the word *courtepointe* (quilt) from Diderot and d'Alembert's famous *Encyclopédie* certainly takes into account the diversity of the term. Of course, patchwork can fulfil many roles, going far beyond a rectangular bedspread made of squares of coloured fabric. Clothing, curtains, hangings and carpets are all proof of this. Although it is often intended to look beautiful, it can also be a symbol of identity, conformity or protest or a reflection of economic, social or political conditions.

As a means of affirming identity, the quilts made by the Amish communities of Pennsylvania reflect their religious beliefs to a degree: their geometric designs are characterized by simplicity and precision. Those made by the women of Pakistan or Gujarat favour bold colours, with tiny mirrors sewn on to reflect the light and keep bad luck away. In northern Vietnam and southern China, the minority peoples of the mountain regions take great pride in their traditional clothing and textile designs. Colours and motifs, in both patchwork and embroidery, function rather like signposts that can be followed from village to village. The reverse appliqué panels called *molas*, created by the Guna women of Panama, are another unmistakeable symbol of cultural identity.

Patchwork styles may also change to reflect economic conditions or trade policies. For instance, in the late 17th century, a law that forbade the importation of printed fabrics from India into French ports encouraged clothmakers from the Rhône-Alpes region, Rouen and Nantes to produce floral fabrics known as *indiennes*, whose offcuts were recycled into patchwork. The same situation led to a contemporary boom in quilts in Great Britain and the Netherlands too. In the USA during the Great Depression, flour bags and feedsacks were often printed with attractive motifs that could be incorporated into quilts.

For a long period in Japan, cotton was a rare and expensive imported material, sparingly used and restricted mostly to the upper classes. Even the tiniest scraps of fabric were gathered by rag-pickers who resold them, travelling from village to village. These were patched together to form new items using an appliqué-like technique known as *boro*; this remains a creative way to give new life to mended textiles.

More generally, the technique of patchwork is a great fit for a culture of recycling, since it is a form of sustainable consumption that reuses rather than throwing away. This time-honoured practice is now more relevant than ever at a time when many are calling for reduced consumption of resources, with the aim of benefiting the environment.

Patchwork may well have been popularized during the Renaissance by the theatrical character Harlequin. Originally a poverty-stricken delivery man, employed by a Venetian tailor, he found himself with no money for a carnival costume. Imagination won the day, however, when his mother gathered up scraps of fabric from his employer and stitched them into the suit of patchwork lozenges now associated with the name Harlequin. Since then, the figure of Harlequin with his distinctive outfit has appeared in many forms throughout the world of art, from theatre to painting.

When colonial missionnaries were attempting to convert indigenous populations, the preachers' wives would sometimes teach reading and writing to local women, along with patchwork and other sewing techniques. In this way, Western-style patchwork was absorbed into a range of global textile traditions, stretching around the world from Pakistan to Hawaii.

In other cases, the technique can be used subversively, to express rebellion or lack of compliance. The US has a long tradition of protest quilts, supporting causes such as the abolition of slavery, temperance movements, or women's suffrage. Some of these, known as fundraising quilts, were sold at auction and the profits donated to charitable associations. Other quilts are commemorative in nature, the best known probably being the AIDS Memorial Quilt, first displayed on the National Mall in Washington DC in 1987, and which subsequently toured the US. Many 9/11 quilts were made to commemorate the victims of the terrorist attack of 11 September 2001. Other forms of commemorative patchwork include the Asafo flags of Ghana and the appliqué banners of Benin.

Patchwork tends to be a gendered craft, with relatively few men engaging in the practice, although African countries are often exceptions to this. Associated with the female domain, quilts, like all forms of needlework, are works that have taken some time to be granted artistic recognition. They were considered part of the long list of 'women's work', invisible and overlooked, located somewhere between convenience and necessity, art and handicraft. Patchwork is often a collective activity among groups of women, who gather to work on a piece together, particularly during the quilting stage. Quilting parties or quilting bees in the USA, the *cercles de fermières* of Quebec, women's associations in Bengal, Kyrgyz women's cooperatives, the quilting workshops of Provence, patchwork clubs: in many places across the world, patchwork is a practice that brings women together in a context of social exchange and community.

While some of the works illustrated in this book stem from the distant past, patchwork is not an outmoded craft from a bygone age. The technique has been modernized, freed from its original rules, and owing to its great flexibility, diversity and modest cost, it still has many contemporary practitioners, working both alone and collectively. A number of women artists, including Sonia Delaunay and Louise Bourgeois among others, have used it as a mode of expression and outlet for their imaginations. Compiling an exhaustive list of patchwork artists would be impossible, so numerous are they.

In the world of patchwork, the unexpected exists alongside the everyday, art alongside craft, luxury alongside thrift, and behind the fabrics there is always a goal or message. This book is an attempt to find patterns and similarities in the many motivations that lie behind patchwork and the many roles that it can play, organizing them like a quilter taking out her fabric stash and sorting the scraps by size, colour and material. The journey will move around the world, region by region, highlighting the distinctive local features of the craft while revelling in the universal nature of this wonderful technique.

Page 8
Vasily Vasilyevich Vereshchagin, *Dervishes from Tashkent in festive costumes,* 1870. Oil on canvas, 71 × 47 cm. Tretyakov Gallery, Moscow. Some Sufi dervishes wear multicoloured patchwork robes as a sign of having forsaken the world of wealth and embracing poverty and mysticism.

Above
Louise Bourgeois, *Untitled,* 2006. Cotton fabric, 38.7 × 48.6 cm. Private collection.

In the 1990s, the artist Louise Bourgeois (1911–2010) began to incorporate items of clothing belonging to herself and her friends and family into her sculptures and other works. This became a way for Bourgeois, who comes from a family of Parisian weavers, to connect with her own childhood and turn textiles into a means of visually and emotionally emphasizing her status as a woman in the art world.

TECHNIQUES

In his workshop in Miskolc, Hungary, Zoltán cuts out pieces of wool felt that will be appliquéd to a traditional herdsman's coat or *cifraszür*. 2013.

Patchwork in its simplest sense is a piece of work assembled from patches of fabric. Americans also use the term 'pieced work.' Most frequently, the individual pieces are sewn together on the reverse side using invisible stitches or close overedge stitching. In contrast, in the style known as crazy quilting, the connecting seams are often emphasized with embroidery stitches and turned into a feature. Most patchwork is planned out in advance and completed stage by stage, usually in individual blocks or rows.

Appliqué is the technique of stitching fabric pieces to a base support. A wide range of materials can be appliquéd: fabric, leather, plastics, knits, lace, ribbons, braids and more. The technique can also be applied to three-dimensional objects. There are two styles: turned edge appliqué, in which the cut edges are turned over before they are stitched down, and raw edge appliqué, in which they are not. The choice of technique depends on the materials used and the finish desired. With silk, cotton, velvet, jersey or another fabric that frays, turned edges are usually preferred. With felt, fulled wool or leather, they are not necessary. Tricks to make the appliqué process easier include double-sided iron-on adhesive sheets or a lightly pasted paper template.

Reverse appliqué is an extension of the technique described above. Several layers of fabric in different colours are arranged on top of each other. The motif is drawn on the topmost layer, then cut away to allow the layers below to show through. The complexity of the motif and the number of colours used can vary. The technique usually incorporates turned edges, as seen in the *molas* of Panama and the Hmong collars and belts of Vietnam. If raw edges are used instead, stitching is added to prevent fraying. The two versions can also be combined, with the choice ultimately down to the maker, depending on whether their focus is on aesthetics, cost, speed or solidity. The selected style will often fit the sewing traditions of the social,

cultural or religious group with whom the work originates, but rule-breaking always remains an option.

Quilting traditionally involves three layers of fabric: the decorative top, the plainer backing, and the filling or batting in between, which creates warmth and volume. Technically speaking, quilting is the process used to join the layers together.

Fabrics of all kinds can be used for patchwork, ranging from heavy (felt or woollens) to lightweight (silk, gauze, synthetics). They can even include fur or fish skin, as in eastern Siberia, or leather, raffia and plastic, as in the Democratic Republic of the Congo. An understanding of the textiles used is vital in order to know how best to sew them together. Very fine or lightweight fabrics may require the addition of interfacing. Using fabrics with a similar weight and texture can make assembly easier, but in the crazy quilt style, rules can easily be broken.

Templates or patterns are useful for cutting out the fabric pieces. They can be made from cardboard or plastic, and may include a seam allowance or not. Simple templates can be made from a piece of paper folded into four, or a plate or box, perhaps. Sometimes they can be inverted or avoided completely by drawing directly onto the fabric. For designs with intricate cut-out details (Chinese appliqué, Hawaiian Star quilts), the template may be pasted in place with removable adhesive. Sometimes a larger template is used to check the size of completed blocks and find out whether any resizing is needed. In addition, the template can be used to sort fabric pieces by size and calculate the total quantity required.

In an encampment near Lake Song Köl in Kyrgyzstan, Aïgul makes a rug (*kurak shyrdak*). She draws the pattern on the felt with chalk, freehand, then uses a sharp blade to cut through multiple layers of fabric, following the chalk lines. The cut-out shapes in different colours will then be arranged edge to edge and stitched together. 2014.

This page, from top to bottom:
In Rajasthan, India, a woman uses a heavy needle to quilt a three-layered bedcover, 2010.

In a workshop in Uzbekistan, a woman cuts out pieces for a patchwork bedspread, 2018.

In Bamako, Mali, one craftsman cuts pieces of polished cotton (bazin), while another stitches stitches strips of fabric together and a third adds appliqué braid to a garment, 2016.

Opposite, above and below:
At Guna Yala in Panama, Guna women sew *molas*, reverse appliqué panels that are traditionally added to their blouses, 2006.

Cutting may be done on the right or wrong side of the fabric, depending on the textile. Even when the pieces are very small, the grain of the fabric must be respected. The colour of fabrics such as velvet, fur, leather, wool or silk varies according to the grain of the fabric, so care must be taken, unless a deliberately mismatched effect is desired. Marking of shapes before cutting requires precision, organization and a minimum of equipment, which could range from simple charcoal to wipe-clean tailor's chalk. A measuring tape or ruler of some kind is also required. The cutting tool may be a blade, a pair of scissors, a rotary cutter or even a laser cutter for semi-industrial products.

Stitches can be done by hand or by machine, and will vary according to the chosen technique. For patchwork, invisible stitching on the reverse is generally used. When left visible, the stitching becomes a key part of the work (*bojagi*, Kuba cloth, crazy quilts) and is often deliberately emphasized. For appliqué, a range of stitches can be used on turned or raw edges: herringbone stitch, stem stitch, satin stitch, blanket or buttonhole stitch, chain stitch and couching, which is particularly common in Chinese appliqué. The fastest technique is generally machine zigzag or satin stitch.

Quilting, which can involve a range of techniques, is usually done by hand once the rest of the piece is finished. Used as a way of adding relief or warmth to a bedcover or throw, on a garment it may be purely decorative. Quilting is frequently done by stretching the textile over a wooden frame. For intricate styles of quilting, an embroidery hoop may be used, as in the case of the *boutis* of Provence. Indian *kantha*, meanwhile, are often laid out on the ground for quilting. The most common filling is cotton or polyester wadding, but old bedlinen, used fabric, silk waste, down feathers or even dried grasses can be used. The quilting process is often a group activity.

Finishes are important. They increase the visual appeal of the work, and add solidity, neatness and longevity. Binding, piping, fringing, frills and lining are among the finishing techniques that can be used. Embroidery can also be used to add sequins, buttons, tassels or beads. The choice of backing fabric may also be interesting. If cloth is in short supply, a backing can be made from pieces of recycled fabric (Indian *ralli* and *kantha*, Uzbek hangings). Some quilts are even backed with a second patchwork. Alternatively, a backing may be deliberately omitted, as in the case of the Kyrgyz *shyrdak* or Korean *bojagi*.

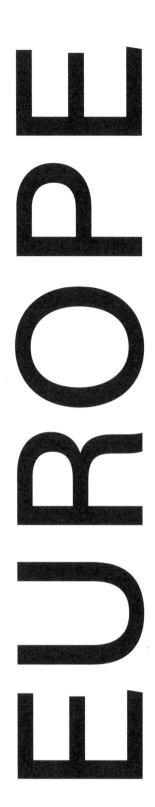

EUROPE

Culcitra punctum. This is what the Romans called a padded bedcover stuffed with straw or feathers. This term later became the English term 'quilt' and the French term *courtepointe*. In addition to bedding, quilting was used to make padded undergarments that could be worn beneath armour, to make it more comfortable, or padded doublets, such as the one made for Charles de Blois in the 14th century, now in the Musée des Tissus in Lyons. Appliqué, meanwhile, was regularly used to decorate banners and military standards.

The oldest surviving patchwork quilt is Swedish; it was probably made for the marriage of a German princess at the beginning of the 14th century. The harsh winters that struck Europe during the 17th and 18th centuries meant that quilted, lined and padded garments were worn by all classes, while wall hangings and bedspreads provided vital insulation. Cotton being rare and other fabrics expensive, poorer people were obliged to gather rags to make blankets. Patching and mending was part of daily life for many, especially women. Nevertheless, practicality and thrift were not the only reasons for using these techniques: patchwork, appliqué and quilting were regularly used to produce luxury items.

From traditional folk costumes to the decorative whims of the wealthy, from the Provençal *boutis* to the Sicilian *trapunto*, the two-tone costumes of Harlequins, clowns and other performers, Europe has no shortage of magnficent patchwork treasures to enjoy.

FRANCE

COURTEPOINTES

Quilts, blankets, bedspreads, table runners, mantel cloths, church banners: a whole array of modest *courtepointes* (patchworks) were designed, stitched and embroidered by anonymous French seamstresses in the 19th and early 20th centuries. Some hailed from the Auvergne region, others from mountain areas, but all of these women were skilful and thrifty.

The level of creativity involved in these modest creations has never been widely acknowledged. Making do with the little one had and setting one's bare feet down on a cozy rug in the morning, even if it was made with pieces of old overcoat, was a source of justifiable pride and a luxury in itself. Brown, grey, black, flecked, striped or herringbone woollens, taken from frock coats, capes, greatcoats, morning coats and jackets, as well as old military uniforms, provided the raw material for many of these items.

Every step in the process was important: gathering rags, sorting them, preparing them, perhaps swapping them with a neighbour, then choosing a style to work in, arranging the colours and deciding on the order in which to sew the pieces together. For this domestic artform, the hardest task is often to keep working until the item is completed

Middle-class women, meanwhile, made rugs, table covers and doilies for side tables, following the fashions of the time. Women's magazines had a wide circulation and often published sewing ideas, encouraging even reluctant seamstresses to begin making a quilt. Patches could be cut from plain or brocaded silks, ribbons, jacquards, damasks, smooth or crushed velvets, silk ties, remnants of dresses, furnishing fabrics or even samples gleaned from an upholsterer.

Contemporary collectors also seek out patchwork produced by another category of women who devoted themselves to this type of work: nuns and novices. They would often produce church banners or altar cloths in their own distinct style.

Courtepointes could vary hugely in shape and size, from a large bedcover to a small table mat. They could be round or oval, rectangular, square or hexagonal. The most traditional style consisted of geometrically shaped pieces sewn together on the reverse, similar to the quilting methods seen in the English-speaking world.

One of the most striking *courtepointe* designs is the *langue de chat* or 'cat's tongue' quilt. The scallop-shaped pieces are cut from felted woollens that will not fray, and are sometimes edged with blanket stitch to emphasize their shape. The pieces are sewn together at the base, leaving the 'tongue' loose, and arranged in an overlapping pattern, radiating from a central point, which is often covered with a medallion. Popularized by magazines, this style is found mainly in Auvergne – in the *départements* of Puy-de-Dôme, Haute-Loire and Cantal – and Ardèche.

Above and opposite (detail): Patchwork wedding bedspread with the central monogram 'MP'. 195 wool squares embroidered with motifs and symbols of rural life are sewn together with embroidery stitches and edged with a fringe. 160 × 180 cm. Cantal, France. Michel Perrier Collection.

Overleaf, left: Detail of a bedspread made from squares of used woollen fabric embroidered with suns and stars. The seams are hidden by feather stitch embroidery. 95 × 145 cm. Auvergne, France. Michel Perrier Collection.

Overleaf, right: Detail of a knitted wool blanket, composed of 286 squares with 7 cm sides. 90 × 180 cm. France. Tuulikki Chompré Collection.

More imaginative still are round quilts that fan out from a central motif, and so-called crazy quilts, which are made from irregularly shaped scraps. Some quilts were made solely from handkerchiefs, badges or ties, while others were embroidered with fleur-de-lis motifs, dogs or cats. Sewing techniques varied according to the materials used and the maker's imagination. The pieces were sewn together or appliquéd, by hand or machine, framed with a border of 'cat's tongues', a scalloped 'tie tips' edge or a woollen fringe.

Coarse or shabby woollen cloth could be enhanced with multicoloured embroidery that disguised worn areas and introduced colour. Seams could be embroidered with feather stitch or herringbone stitch. For an imaginative touch, a star, a cross, a flower, or an animal could be embroidered in the centre of the square or where four pieces overlapped.

Collector Michel Perrier, who prefers to say that he 'rescues textiles', loves these *courtepointes*. To him, each of these fabric mosaics tells a story, always personal and often moving. Although they have long been neglected, they are truly worthy of a place in the pantheon of textile art.

Left:
Detail of a bedside rug in wool and cotton. Central panel made of rows of scallop-shaped motifs, embroidered with stars and edged with blanket stitch. Outer border maded from pieces folded into the shape of 'tie tips'. Hemp backing fabric. 65 × 140 cm. France. Michel Perrier Collection.

Right:
Tablecloth. Rectangles of silk, arranged in concentric circles. Silk tabs folded into the shape of 'tie tips' radiate from the centre and form a border for each circular row. Unlined. Diameter 128 cm. Auvergne, France. Michel Perrier Collection.

WINDOW QUILT

A *vane à fenêtre* or 'window' quilt is a style of quilt often found in the French region of Provence. It consists of an elegant printed fabric that forms a border around a central 'window'. Sometimes these central panels are made up of a mosaic of small pieces, offcuts from garments or remnants salvaged from old clothes.

All kinds of fabric prints, geometrics, florals and stripes can used in this design. While a simple gathered rectangle of fabric can make a skirt, cutting a more elaborate garment such as a jacket leaves plenty of offcuts behind. Sewn together, they can be used as a lining fabric; cut into patches, they become a quilt.

This quilt's 'window' is made from small right-angled triangles, cut and stitched in pairs to form squares, then built up into blocks of four, eight and so on. The colourful pattern resembles the print fabric known in Provence as *indiano piso*, with multicoloured flowers scattered on a pale ground. Other popular print styles included *bonnes herbes*, with dense wildflowers and grasses on a bronze ground; *ramoneur*, with the same motifs on a dark ground; and *bâtons rompus*, a geometric arrangement of stylized plants.

In 17th-century France, there was a thriving fashion for *indiennes*, light floral cottons printed in India for the European market. In order to protect the French textile industry, however, the import of these fabrics was banned in 1686. As a result, however, Indian florals become even more sought-after, and were sold on the black market. Only Marseilles, a free port, was temporarily excluded from the ban.

By 1759, when the import ban was lifted, workshops producing printed cottons, scarves and upholstery fabrics had spread throughout France. Initially, as in India, the printing was done with wooden blocks, using as many blocks as there were colours. Next,

the manufacturers began using copper plates, producing detailed designs, and then switched to copper rollers, which allowed for mass production at a low cost, albeit at the expense of colour: prints became largely monochrome. Some manufacturers, including the famous firm of Christophe Philippe Oberkampf, based in Jouy-en-Josas, near Versailles, succeeded in producing top-of-the-range fabrics using wooden blocks at the same time as printing cheaper products with a roller.

Textiles are usually dated by analysing the materials used, the style of the motifs, their quality and provenance. The broad range of fabrics in the quilt shown here include

Above:
'Window' quilt. 864 right-angled triangles of cotton and silk, with 4.5 cm sides, sewn into blocks of 8. Broad yellow cotton piqué border. Backing of *ikat*-style *siamoise* print. 127 × 147 cm. Probably from the Drôme region, France, late 18th or early 19th century. Michel Perrier Collection.

block-printed, copperplate and resist-dyed textiles, suggesting a date from the late 18th or early 19th century. It is backed with a linen and cotton *siamoise* print, bearing a blue and white *ikat*-style design.

COMTADINE SKIRT

***Coutihoun pèço emé pèço* is the Provençal for 'patchwork petticoat'. In fact, the garment shown below is not a separate petticoat but the lining of a skirt of *indienne* printed cotton, featuring small flowers scattered on a white ground. Made in around 1860, the skirt would have belonged to a *grangère comtadine*, that is to say to the mistress of a large farm in the Comtat Venaissin region, near Avignon.**

A traditional Provençal skirt is made up of three layers: a cotton or silk fabric on the outside, an inexpensive lining fabric and, between them, a layer of cotton or silk wadding. When quilted together, these layers form a skirt capable of resisting the cold mistral winds. The basic shape is a large rectangle, closed by a seam and gathered into a belt with flat or cannon pleats. The seamed side includes an opening that allows the skirt to be taken on and off; this would usually have been hidden under the ever-present apron.

The striking lining of the skirt shown here is made of rectangular patches sewn edge to edge, probably pieces of old skirts or offcuts from a tailor's workshop. The arrangement of the eighty pieces is far from random: the colours are alternated and the patterns carefully chosen, including checks, polka dots, small all-overs and stripes. The resulting design recalls the terracotta tiles of a Provençal farmhouse. The skirt is held together by chequerboard quilting, which runs diagonal to the rest of the design.

Quilting is traditionally a key element of Provençal identity and features on men's clothing, such as waistcoats, women's clothing, including skirts, bodices and jackets, and on bedcovers for the home. The techniques may well have been imported by the Crusaders and these items are regularly recorded in inventories from the 16th century onwards.

Left:
Reverse side of a Provençal skirt, showing its patchwork cotton lining. H. 86 cm, full width 280 cm. Vaucluse, France, c. 1860. Conservatoire du Costume Comtadin, Pernes-les-Fontaines.

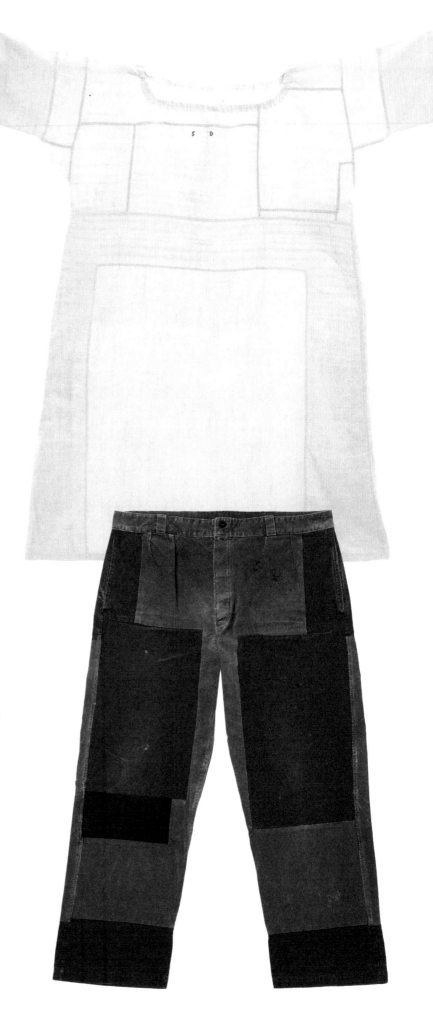

UPCYCLING AND VISIBLE MENDING

Whatever the term used to describe them, many mending techniques have similarities to patchwork and may even be where its origins lie. Visible mending may also incorporate other sewing techniques such as embroidery.

Depending on the type of garment, a maker might opt for a clearly visible repair that serves to reinforce a worn area of fabric, or alternatively, seek to conceal the wear and tear by stitching a piece of fabric underneath, as identical as possible, so that the repair remains discreet. Mending of this kind was never exclusively confined to women; many men also took care of their clothes, particularly their work clothes, in an era when people bought little and threw away less.

An unassuming garment, the white blouse originating from the Berry region is made up of remnants salvaged from old shirts or sheets. The seventeen pieces are carefully arranged at right angles and sewn using flat felled seams. The distinction between the linen and cotton pieces creates slight differences in shade. The small size of the fragments suggests extreme frugality. If this is a monastic shirt, wthe patching could be viewed as a sign of austerity, even humility. From a purely aesthetic point of view, this shirt can be compared to the white Korean *bojagi* (see p. 150).

The blue work trousers are a patched-up piece of industrial clothing. Did they belong to a labourer, a fisherman, a farmer? Only the stains and the wear and tear can answer this question. The clearly visible mending proudly displays the working status of the garment's wearer. These pieces are proof of careful patching, carried out by a skilful and thrifty owner who recycled old clothes.

The short jacket, meanwhile, is a survivor which must have accompanied more than

one woman to the fields. It has been patched up many times, but always from the inside, so that it wouldn't show. The sleeves, front, back, and collar have almost entirely been remade, discreetly lined with scraps of ecru, indigo or printed fabrics, in order to reinforce the delicate and worn out parts.

The peasant skirt below is so worn that it is remarkable to find it in one piece. In a former life, it was pretty, hand-sewn in a solid silk and linen filoche weave, carefully gathered into a belt with cannon pleats. Many years later, when the fabric was worn thin, small patches were added to cover the holes and attempt a final rescue. Shirt fabric, trouser fabric, chambray, ticking, black sateen – anything available has been stitched into this skirt. Stylistically, it resembles the Japanese mending technique known as *boro* (see pp. 152–157).

This page and opposite: A selection of used and patched garments made from cotton and linen fabrics. Shirt (*opposite, above*), worker's trousers (*opposite, below*), reverse side of jacket (*above*) and underskirt (*right*). France. Tuulikki Chompré and Catherine Legrand Collections.

GREAT BRITAIN

MEDALLION QUILT

The central medallion of this quilt is made from a Persian print fabric, in a similar style to the Indian prints that were extremely fashionable in Britain in the early 19th century. It depicts a pair of colourful birds watching over a nest full of eggs, perched on a branch adorned with flowers and fruits, an image of Eden-like fruitfulness. The octagonal medallion sits at the centre of a large grid made up of elongated hexagon motifs.

In fact, this quilt features a range of geometric shapes: squares, elongated hexagons, diamonds, triangles, octagons and even circles, appliquéd around the edge. The colourful print fabrics have been carefully arranged, so that those with a lighter ground run horizontally and those with a dark ground vertically. Quilts with a central medallion are a tradition that flourished in Great Britain from the 17th century onwards, but only rarely made its way across the Atlantic. These medallion quilts were accompanied by Persian embroidery, bouquets or fruit motifs cut from Indian fabrics and appliquéd using buttonhole stitch.

The back of these bedcovers reveals another striking feature. The seamstresses used paper templates for each patch, stitching the fabric around them. They cut out as many templates as fabric patches, making use of magazines, letters, leaflets or any other kind of paper that was sufficiently thick. This method has proved to be a gold mine for historians, who have discovered valuable facts from the cut-up papers. The template was the same shape as the final patch, without the allowance for seams. Placed on the back of the fabric, and sometimes lightly pasted in place, it acted as a guide when cutting out the patch. A few extra millimetres of fabric were left around the template, allowing the excess to be folded down over the paper edge and then tacked in place. These paper-lined patches were then delicately stitched together. Very precise and allowing the use of small scraps of fabric, this method was suited to a time when printed cottons were a rare commodity.

The history of textiles in Great Britain bears a strong resemblance to that of France (see p. 24); as early as 1700, there was a ban on the import of printed cottons from India, in order to protect local weavers of wool and linen. As in France, this only increased the appetite for these contraband fabrics, which were hugely popular for both clothes and interiors. The British textile industry therefore adapted to meet the growing demand for printed fabrics. British quilts have always tended to include a huge variety of fabrics, with imported Indian cloth used alongside chintz, prints and calendered cotton made in the UK.

Right:
Medallion quilt, attributed to Mary Gibbs. 216 × 240 cm. England, 1812. Christopher Wilson-Tate Collection.

Overleaf:
Detail of a quilt with motif of 3 cm-sided cubes in plain and patterned silks. On the front side (*left*), the tacking stitches are still visible. From the back (*right*), it can be seen that each silk diamond has been folded and stitched around a paper template. UK. Catherine Legrand Collection.

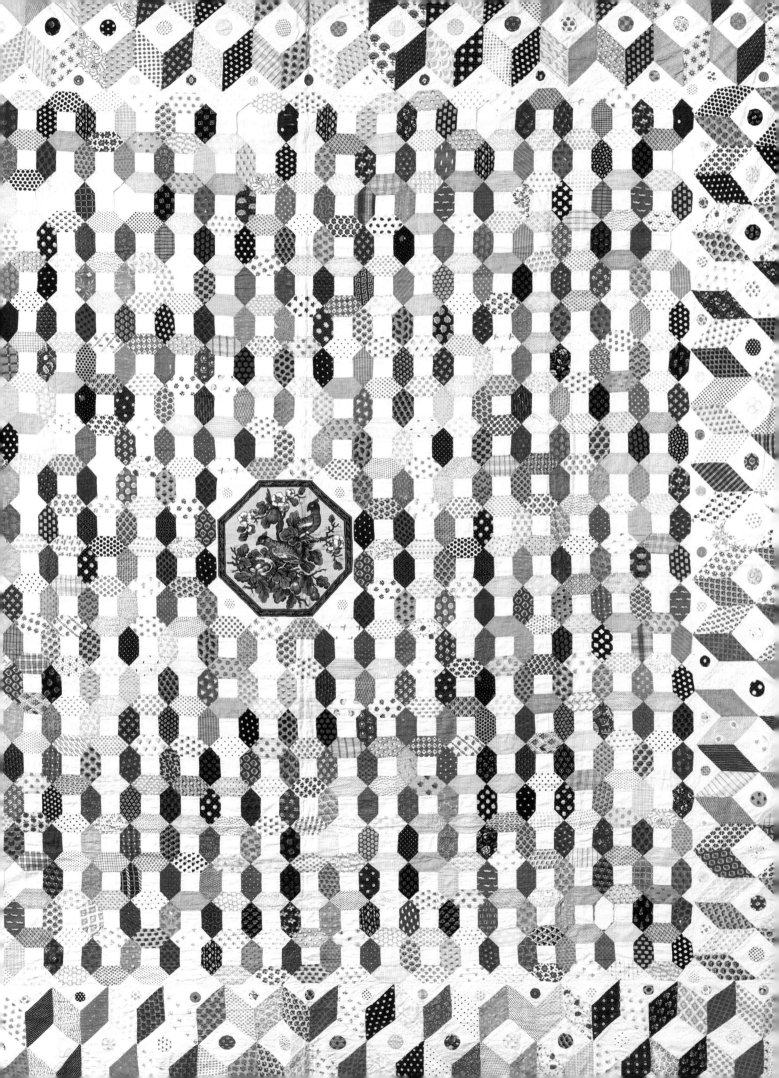

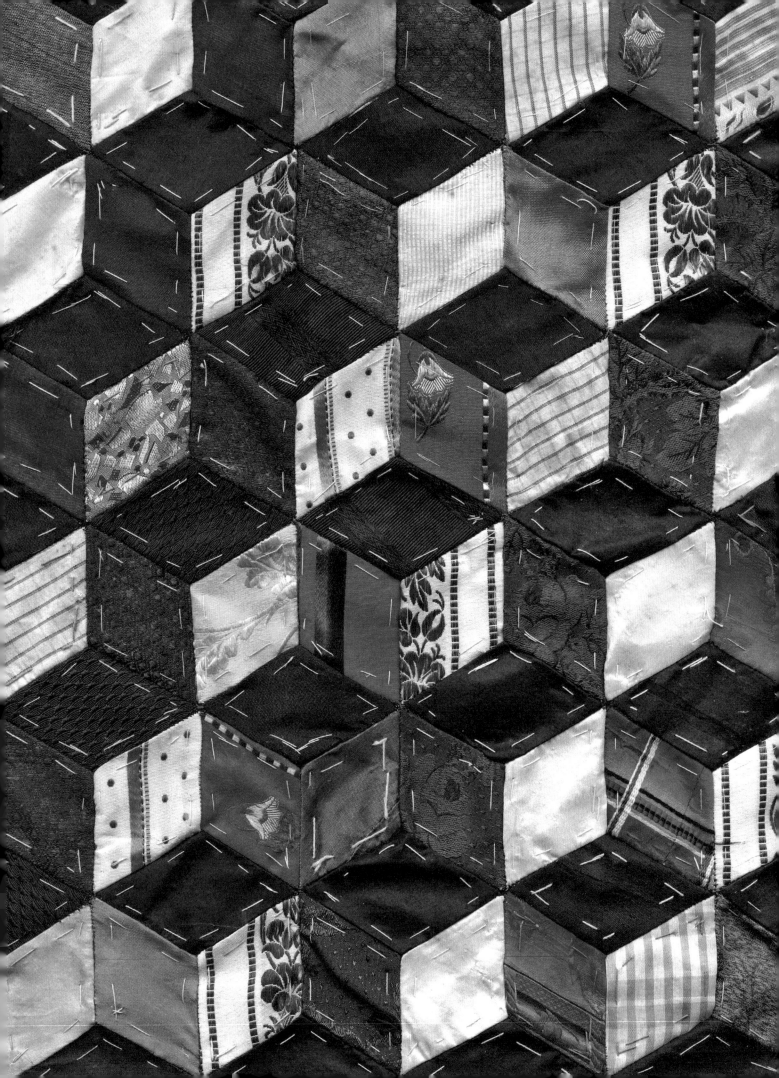

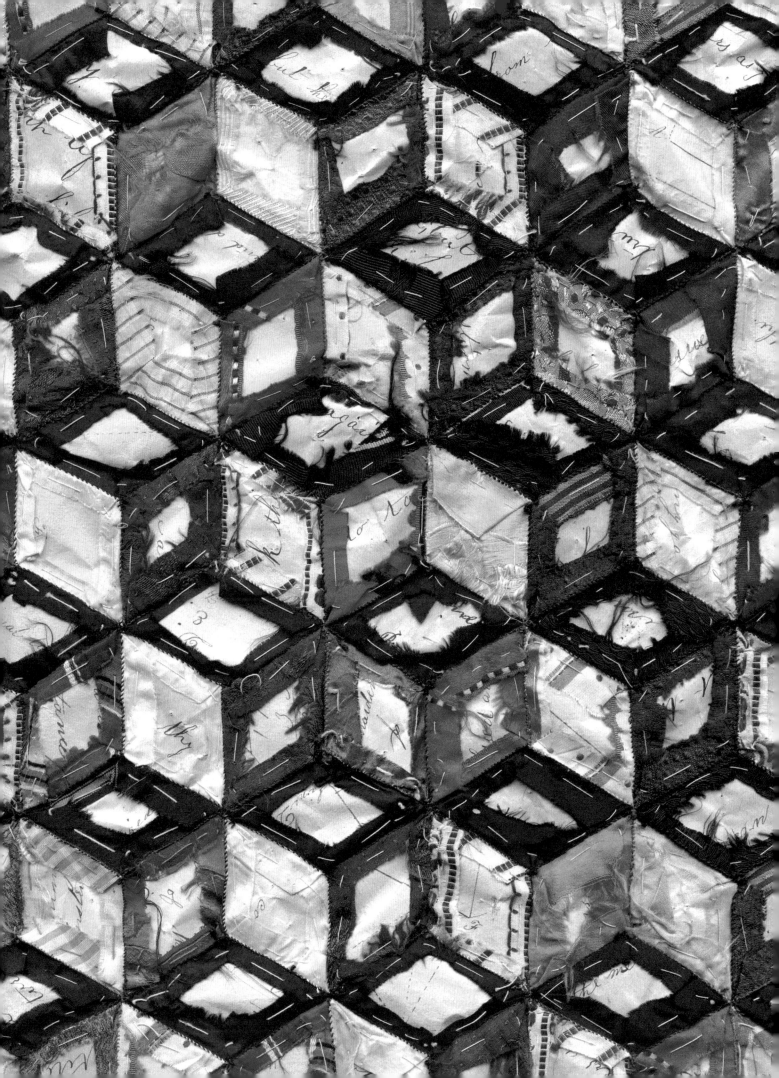

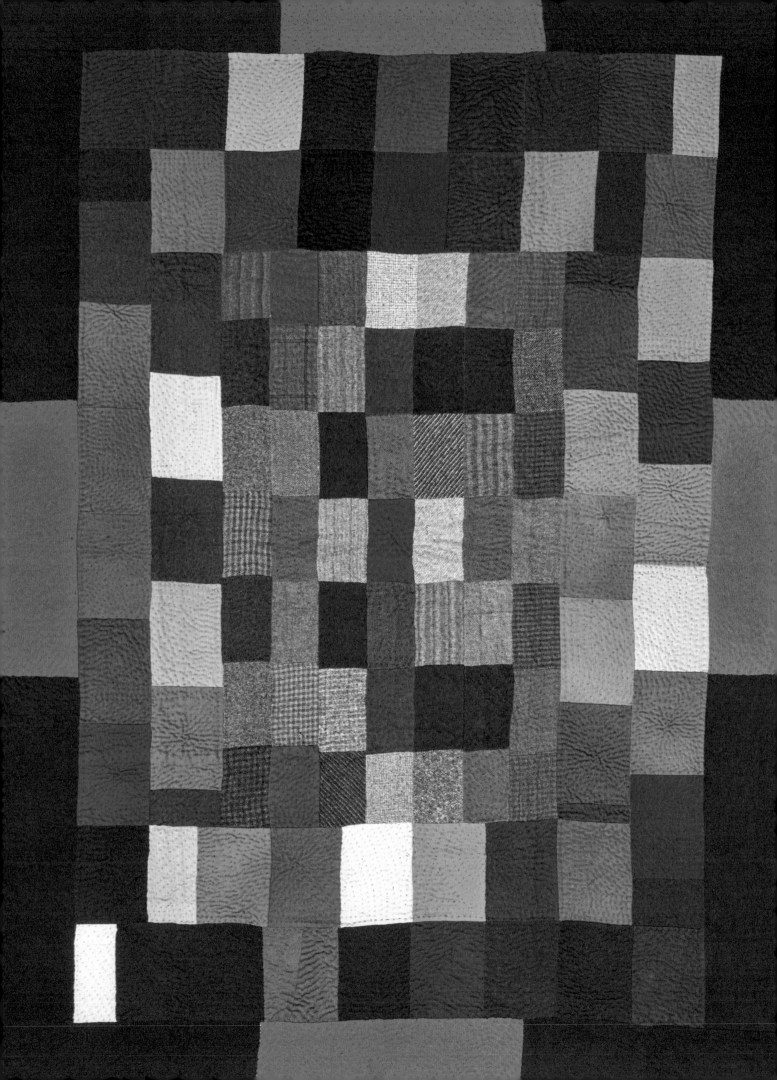

HIRED MAN'S QUILT

From the mid-19th century, along the many waterways of Wales, the cloth mills specialized in weaving brightly coloured flannels and woollens. A tradition of hand-crafted bedlinen and household items also developed there. The clientele were wealthy families, who appreciated the art of quilting, and came from a social class in which sewing and embroidery formed an integral part of the education of girls.

In Wales, seasonal workers enjoyed special status. Going from farm to farm as required, day labourers never went anywhere without a blanket or quilt, often a patchwork made of scraps of wool and remnants of old blankets, made with the frugality and imagination that rural life so often demanded.

During this period, many Welsh people emigrated to America, particularly to Pennsylvania, where their skills as coal miners were in high demand. They took with them only a few possessions, including their patchwork quilts. The geometric designs of Welsh quilts, decorated with stars and wide stripes, along with the style of quilting and colour schemes, share many similarities with those of Pennsylvania's Amish communities.

The quilt shown opposite would not look out of place on the walls of a museum, next to a work by the Bauhaus artist Josef Albers. The colours are arranged harmoniously, and the composition is both irregular and carefully structured.

Opposite:
Hired man's quilt. Used woollen fabrics. 177 × 209 cm. Wales, 1890. Charles-Édouard de Broin Collection.

Right:
Vintage postcard depicting a sexton, whose job it was to care for the grounds of a church, pictured with his scythe. Wales, early 20th century.

THE SEXTON

SWEDEN

KJOLSÄCK

This loose pocket or pouch formed part of a Swedish woman's traditional costume from medieval times until the mid-19th century. It is said that avoid falling asleep during long sermons in church, women would put a few sage leaves, ginger roots or cloves into their *kjolsäck* to wake themselves up, sometimes with the addition of a crust of bread on which they could nibble discreetly during the service.

Originally, the *kjolsäck* was simply a small bag that hung loose from a belt. Before the advent of clothes with built-in pockets, it was a safe place for storage, which a woman could reach by folding back her apron and slipping her hand into the opening of her skirt. Long since fallen from everyday use, it survived as part of Swedish folk costume and became an attractive accessory, while retaining its utilitarian function. The tie cord was replaced by a silver or brass hook fastening at the top, while the fabric pouch was elongated into a pear shape.

Whether decorated with embroidery, patchwork or appliqué, the *kjolsäck* allowed a woman to show off her sewing skills and indicated her social status and region. Sometimes the pocket virtually became an identity card, adorned with its owner's initials and date of birth.

The majority of pouches were adorned with embroidery, but some incorporated mosaics of appliqué fabric, always symmetrically arranged. Triangular and diamond-shaped pieces were cut from felted wool, remnants from clothing or military uniforms, combined with calfskin or suede, chosen for its suppleness and texture. The pieces were then arranged edge to edge.

An alternative style of *kjolsäck* was decorated with raw-edge appliqué motifs cut from felted wool. Stylized plant or animal shapes, in red or green, were stitched onto a dark background and outlined with pewter braid. This Viking-inspired decorative style was often practised in the Hälsingland region.

The *kjolsäck* was given strength and solidity by its backing and edging, which was cut from animal hide, a widely available material.

Above:
Belt pouch (*kjolsäck*). Woollen cloth, calfskin and embroidery. Brass hook. H. approx. 25 cm. Sweden, 1826. Nordiska Museum, Stockholm.

Below:
Belt pouch (*kjolsäck*). Woollen cloth appliqué, pewter thread. Calfskin back. H. approx. 25 cm. Sweden, 1810–1820. Nordiska Museet, Stockholm.

WEDDING PILLOWS

During a marriage ceremony in a Swedish Evangelical Lutheran church, the future spouses traditionally sat on specially made cushions or *dyna*. Always made in pairs, often embroidered with the initials of the couple and/or the year of the wedding, they were then carefully kept at home, furnishing a bench or displayed on either side of the window in the living room.

Their motifs, which often take the form of a chequerboard, wind rose, compass or hourglass, led to the belief, as Anna Maria Claesson suggests in Åsa Wettre's book *Old Swedish Quilts* (1995), that they were generally made by men, such as village tailors or soldiers. In fact, these could easily be the same man, and thus a person well placed to draw on his experience of fashions or events from the wider world.

The cushion was made of a dense woollen fabric called *vadmal*, which does not fray. The colours were those used for military uniforms: red, green, yellow, indigo. Called *skarvsöm* in Swedish, the patchwork technique used to assemble the pieces was similar to that used for the pockets shown opposite. Two pieces would be sewn together using overedge stitch, with piping inbetween, often made from a thin strip of soft chamois, tanned sheepskin or calfskin. Hardwearing sheep- or calfskin would be used for the back of the cushion. The corners were sometimes embellished with tassels made from scraps of fabric. Feathers, wool or straw were used as a filling.

LAPPTÄCKE

Jan Troell's film, *The Emigrants* (1971), based on a novel by Vilhelm Moberg, offered a memorable portrayal of life in the Swedish countryside in the 19th century. Poor harvests, famine, unemployment: the fictional Nilsson family shared the same fate as nearly a million Swedish farmers who were driven by poverty into exile in America. Many of them may have carried in their luggage wrapped in an old quilt made by a grandmother.

Indeed, the origin of Swedish quilts remains unclear. Did the earliest quilts emerge in Sweden or was the craft brought back by emigrants who returned to their homeland? The question is impossible to answer, since any quilt or handcrafted object is the result of a slow process in which necessity is combined with imagination, need generates technique, and fashions and influences also play a role.

The history of Swedish quilting owes a great deal to research done by Åsa Wettre. In her book *Old Swedish Quilts* (1995), Wettre manages to match a name, a face (perhaps a descendant or an heir), a house, a region or an anecdote to many quilts, turning each patchwork into a window on the lives of Swedish people of the 19th century and the first half of the 20th century. The oldest bedcovers in Sweden were probably made from animal skins or felted wool. Later, elegant patchworks or quilted silks adorned the beds of the wealthy classes while rural people slept on straw or even dried kelp, with a flour sack as a blanket. It is likely that old clothes were stitched together to serve as bedding.

The heyday of Swedish quilts coincided with the return of some emigrants to their homeland when industrialization began. The advent of paper manufacture from wood cellulose meant that households were no longer obliged to pass on used fabrics to the

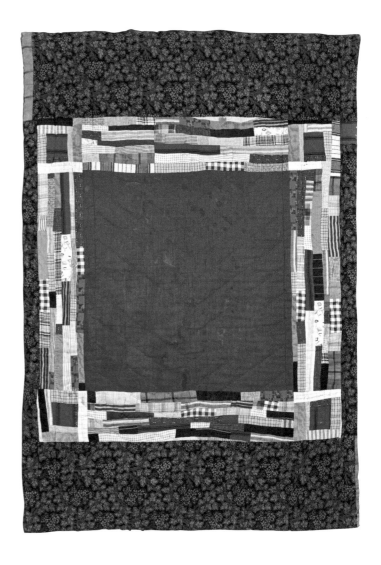

paper industry. Old clothes or worn bedlinen therefore offered a new opportunity for creativity. Shredded into strips and woven together, they became striped rugs. Cut and sewn together, they turned into quilts. The growth of the textile industry provided cotton fabrics to replace flax and hemp. The year 1872 also marked the birth of the robust Scandinavian Husqvarna sewing machine.

The range of quilt motifs used was extensive. One popular example was the Log Cabin, which became established in Sweden before reaching the USA. Men would cut the pieces, then women would sort the

Above:
Quilt (*lapptäcke*). Village of Habo, Sweden, c. 1900–1920. Former collection of Åsa Wettre, Västergötlands Museum, Skara.

Opposite:
Central motif of a soldier's quilt (*soldattäcke*), made from serge from old uniforms and military blankets. 168 × 123 cm. Sweden, 1840. Textilmuseet, Borås.

fabrics, separating them into light and dark, then stitching them around a central square, which was often red, to symbolize hearth and home.

The quilt shown above is the work of one man, Bengt Träff, a retired soldier who, like many reservists, was also a tailor. Träff salvaged pieces of woollen cloth in yellow, indigo and red from used uniforms, while the green strips come from army blankets. The composition is lively, and the centre of the wind rose is adorned with the date of the quilt's completion. It is possible to make out a frieze of hearts stitched head-to-tail on the green border, suggesting that the quilt was probably created for a family event.

SAMI TUNIC

The Sami people of Lapland traditionally dressed in reindeer skins, sewn with sinew. Later, wool from Flanders or Britain was traded in the region by Norwegian merchants and was used for tunics that retained the same characteristic shape. The tunic slips over the head and flares out from the waist, cinched with a belt.

The Sami Easter Festival, held in Kautokeino in Norwegian Lapland, brings together Sami people from Sweden, Norway and Finland. It provides the perfect opportunity to see traditional tunics being worn, in place of the modern anoraks that have replaced them for everyday wear. A great variety of traditional styles can be seen: longer ones from the South, some with front openings, others held by a silver brooch, some in undyed grey wool, others in blue or red. All are decorated with raw-edged strips of felted wool, which may be straight or curved. Varying in width, sometimes scalloped, the brightly coloured bands adorn the necklines, cuffs, shoulder seams, hem, and the upper back at shoulder blade level.

It is interesting to compare these tunics with the traditional garments of the Ainu people of Hokkaido (see p. 158), which feature designs around the openings that serve a symbolic role as protective barriers.

SAMI POUCH

These decorative pouches were traditionally used to carry tobacco or other personal items.

Made from soft and supple animal skin, each pouch consists of several pieces: an upper band with two cords of twisted leather running through it, finished with felt tassels; a semicircular front and back; and a side gusset to create volume. The decoration is a mosaic of red, yellow and black felt, often leftover remnants from traditional Sami garments. Deerskin piping inserted between the pieces of fabric creates a design that recalls a leaded stained glass window.

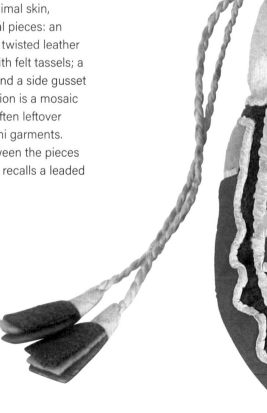

Opposite, far left:
Vintage postcard. Two Sami men wearing traditional costume, including tunics and Four Winds hats.

Opposite, above:
Sami boy's tunic. Wool and cotton with appliqué bands and braid. H. 67 cm. Lapland, c. 1970. Världskulturmuseet, Gothenburg.

Below:
Sami pouch. Woollen fabric and animal skin with drawstring. H. 10.5 cm. Lapland, late 19th century. Nordiska Museet, Stockholm.

Right:
Four Winds hat. Woollen cloth and braid. H. 22 cm. Lapland, c. 1970. Världskulturmuseet, Gothenburg.

FOUR WINDS HAT

The Four Winds hat, known as a *ciehgahpir* in the Sami language, is worn by Sami men from the Kautokeino region, in the far north of Norway. It is said that its shape was copied from that of the headgear worn by Russian sailors and merchants who came to trade in the Norwegian fjords.

The four corners of this square-shaped hat have been elongated into horn-like points, resembling the sails of a windmill. The headband around the bottom is decorated with appliqué braids and woollen bands, either raw-edged or scalloped, and a tassel made of felt. The corners of the hat are often stuffed with goose feathers or reindeer hair.

Although modern textiles now provide better protection from the cold, traditional Sami garments, with their recognizable colours and motifs, remain important symbols of cultural heritage and belonging.

HUNGARY

WAISTCOAT & BOOTS

This style of shearling waistcoat is popular throughout Eastern Europe, from Russia to the Balkans. The one shown opposite comes from Transdanubia in southwest Hungary. Traditionally worn in both winter and summer by men and women, it keeps in warmth without hindering movement. Made from easily available materials, the garment required only a small quantity of sheepskin: two pieces for the front, the back and two shoulder pieces.

The fleecy side of the sheepskin is worn on the inside. The outer side is covered with motifs cut from supple skins dyed green, pink, red and yellow. The designs are cut out using a template, then appliquéd or inlaid. Strips of notched leather adorn the edges. The circular perforations and small holes are punched with an awl. The decorated area is edged with a leather strip with fancy stitching. The bottom of the waistcoat has a border of cut-out semicircles. The V-shaped appliqué motif creates a kind of *trompe-l'oeil* effect that recalls the darts in a fitted cloth waistcoat.

The decoration draws on a highly stylized folk repertoire: hearts, flowers and foliage, and sometimes the initials of the wearer. Identical motifs are used by local wood carvers or painted on decorated chests. Embroidery is added to complete the decoration. In some regions, depending on the local craft traditions, embroidery dominates the inlaid leather motifs.

The men's boots shown above, which were traditionally accompanied by baggy trousers, are worn only on special occasions. Made from very fine leather, they are decorated with patchwork motifs. The traditional patterns – hearts, flowers, petals or ram's horns – are cut from coloured leather and are interlocked. Each cut-out piece generates a reversed pattern, which is used and inlaid in its turn. The arabesques are surrounded by fine embroidery in beige thread. This inlay technique is reminiscent of the decorated sandals and bags produced by the Tuareg people of North Africa (see p. 114).

Left:
Vintage postcard. A German woman from the Siebenburg region of Romanian Transylvania, wearing a sleeveless shearling waistcoat, embroidered with flowers in satin stitch and appliqué motifs in cut-out leather.

Above:
Boots. Dyed leather. H. 40 cm. Former Austro-Hungarian Empire, late 19th century. Catherine Legrand Collection.

Opposite:
Back of a young girl's waistcoat. Shearling, wool and mirrors. 28 × 34 cm. Southern Transdanubia, Hungary, late 19th century. Museum of International Folk Art, Santa Fe.

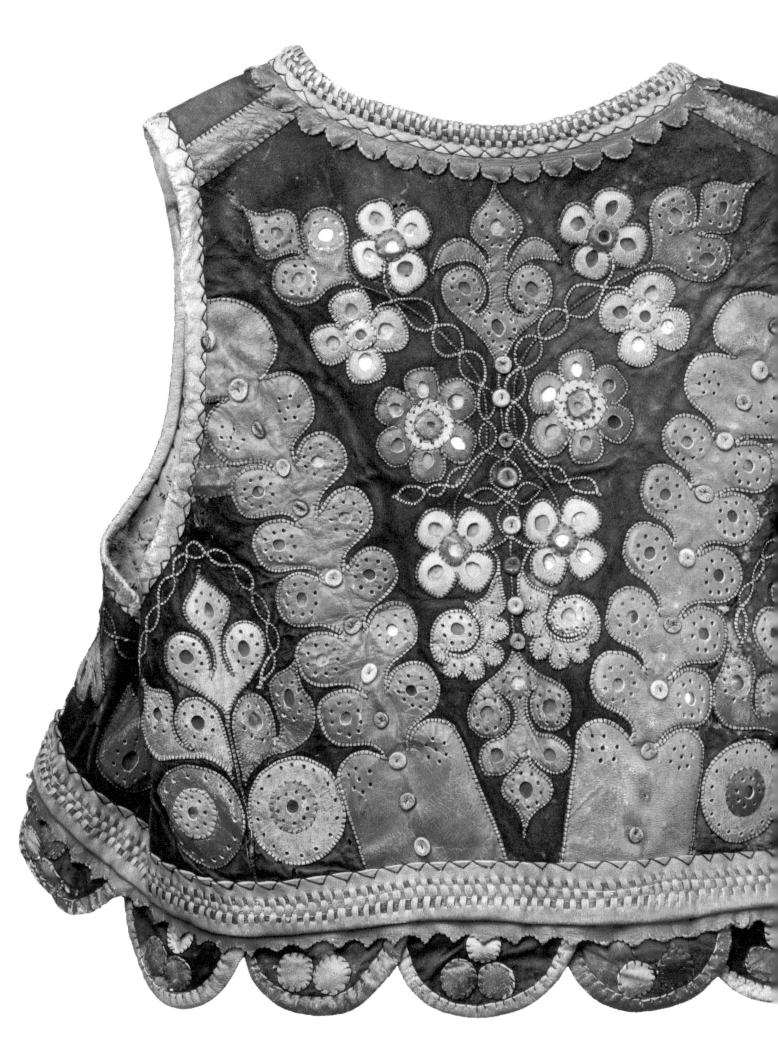

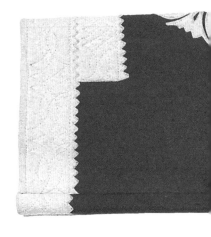

CIFRASZÜR

The *cifraszür*, a coat made from fulled wool, has become a national emblem of Hungary. At the time of the Austro-Hungarian Empire, it was fashionable to wear a *cifraszür* over the shoulder as a sign of cultural identity. In the 19th century, the Hungarian bourgeoisie and aristocracy embraced this iconic garment with peasant origins as a way to distinguish themselves from Austrians and other nationalities.

This coat was originally worn by the cowherds and shepherds of the Puszta, the Hungarian steppe, and also by brigands. Its wool comes from the fleece of the *racka*, a local breed of sheep. Traditionally, weavers (*csapo*) would settle near sheep farms and collect the fleeces. The wool was washed, spun and woven, before being taken to the fulling mills that were built beside rivers. The fulling process made the fabric waterproof, meaning that the *cifraszür* offered protection against bad weather and could even serve as a shelter for sleeping. The sleeves, often sewn shut at the cuffs, could be used as a pockets and for storing tobacco.

Too stiff to wear as a normal coat, the *cifraszür* was thrown over the shoulders, like a cape. This rustic garment was originally undecorated, but as time passed, it was adorned with sumptuous embroidery or appliqué motifs. The garment was archaic in shape, consisting of rectangular pieces cut with raw edges from a felted woollen cloth that did not require hemming or lining. The front and back are made from a single piece, with two sleeves sewn to the body at right angles, two pieces forming the sides, two broad lapels on either side of the opening, an optional small straight collar (for coats in the Széchenyi style) and, on the back, a large square collar which, thanks to the roundels at its corners, could be folded and closed to form a hood.

Often seen displayed for sale at major regional fairs, some of these coats are still made to measure. Zoltán is one of the few tailors who works to order, and specializes in *cifraszür* adorned with appliqué cut-outs. He creates his own designs, making use of different colours of felts and decorative stitching. In his small workshop in Miskolc, in northeastern Hungary, he traces out the pieces with chalk, then cuts them out and stitches them together (see p. 12). His skill lies in the accuracy with which he cuts the openwork motifs that he will then carefully fix in place using a sewing machine. Pinking shears or cutters can make the task easier, but most of the cutting is done by hand, with a pair of small sharp scissors using cardboard templates.

Then the needle of the sewing machine launches into its dance, curving and twisting around the intricate shapes. To make his

Left:
Vintage postcard. Two herdsmen wearing *cifraszür* on the Hungarian steppe.

Opposite:
Child's coat (*cifraszür*). Felted wool cloth. 75 × 58 cm, arm span 114 cm. Hungary. Tuulikki Chompré Collection.

task, the tailor must plan his work. He begins with the smaller pieces: the appliqué motifs for the sleeves, the lapels and the collar are sewn in a precise order. Any other approach would be impractical, as the coat would be too thick and heavy to pass under the presser foot of the sewing machine. In addition to these large, expensive coats, Hungarian craftsmen make smaller items that are more saleable, such as placemats and cushion covers.

In the village of Buzsák, south of Lake Balaton in the Somogy region, seamstresses use another style of appliqué to make tablecloths, handkerchiefs, curtains and blouses decorated with cut-out floral and plant motifs in a plain red cotton. These are tacked, then sewn with small stitches onto a white cotton base. This technique is also used by Slovak seamstresses from Trakovice and Martovce, towns near the Hungarian border and formerly part of the Austro-Hungarian Empire, dissolved in 1920.

Above left:
Place mat. Felted wool. Diameter 25 cm. Hungary. Catherine Legrand Collection.

Above right:
Tablecloth. Cotton. 140 × 140 cm. Buzsák, Hungary. Catherine Legrand Collection.

Opposite:
Detail of a cushion. Wool felt. 45 × 30 cm. Hungary. Catherine Legrand Collection.

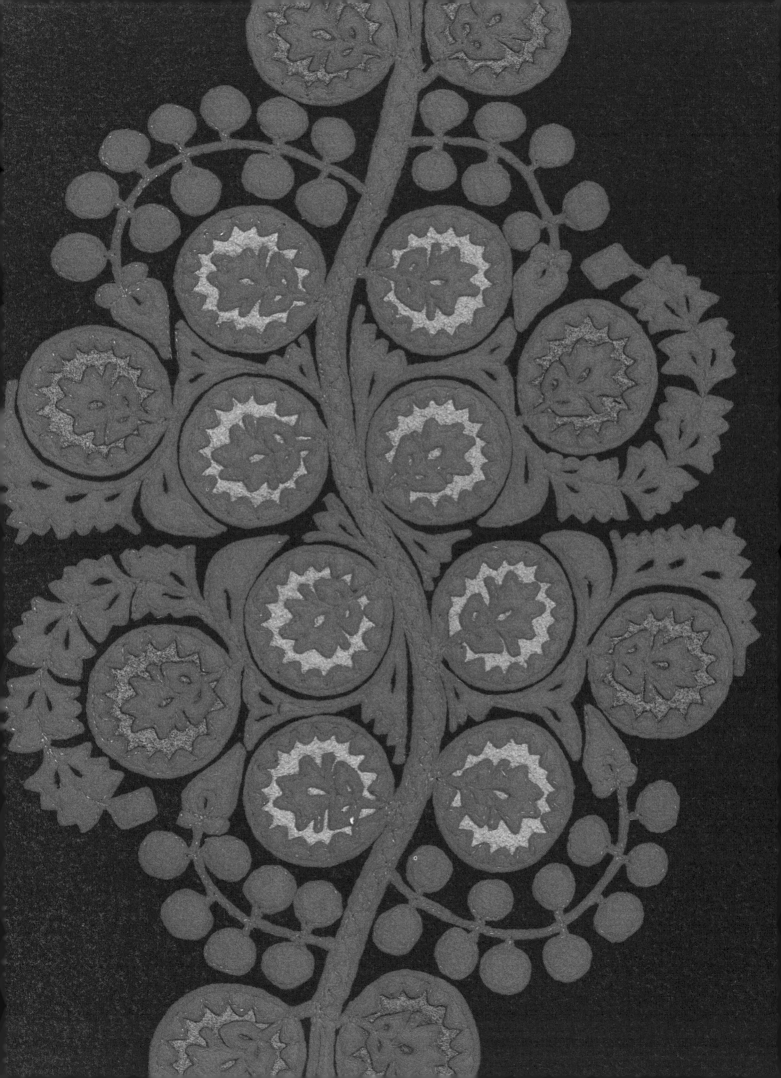

THE NETHERLANDS

FEESTROK

The story of this skirt began in 1943, on the day Adrienne Minette (Mies) Boissevain-van Lennep (1896–1965), a member of the Dutch resistance, was arrested in Amsterdam by German soldiers. Interned at Vught in the Netherlands, then in Ravensbrück concentration camp, she secretly received from her Dutch friends a scarf made of scraps of fabrics belonging to her relatives.

This token of friendship and moral support was not forgotten when she was released in 1945. She became a member of a committee of women who decided to sew symbolic garments that expressed positive concepts such as 'unity in diversity', 'new from old', and 'building from the broken'.

Known as a *feestrok*, 'celebration skirt', *bevrijdingsrok*, 'liberation skirt', or *levensrok*, 'life skirt', this style of patchwork skirt became a social movement in itself. An impressive number of them were specially made, each one bearing the embroidered date of 5 May 1945, the day of the liberation of the Netherlands from Nazi rule. These skirts, all specially registered and numbered, were designed to be worn on national holidays. Although only a few examples remain, preserved by families or museums, they symbolically mark the birth of feminism in the Netherlands and testify to the major role played by women in the Dutch Resistance.

DUTCH QUILTS

It was the age of sea trade. The ships of the Dutch East India Company had already rounded the Cape of Good Hope, followed close behind by those of the French and British East India Companies. In the 18th century, competition for business was fierce. On the quays of Lorient, Nantes, Liverpool, London, Antwerp and Amsterdam, whoever unloaded first could get the best prices for their cargoes of tea, coffee and spices, bales of unbleached muslin and percale, Chinese porcelain, indigo, and much coveted lengths of chintz and Indian floral prints.

The demand for silks began to fall in favour of Indian floral prints. These soon filled the bourgeois homes that were depicted by the painters of the Dutch Golden Age. Bedspreads, hangings and curtains reflected a new love of exoticism, depicting flowers, birds and fruits in brilliant colours. Initially, whole rolls of cloth, lined and quilted, were used to adorn beds. But soon, in the Netherlands and elsewhere, Indian fabrics were appropriated by fashion.

Opposite:
Celebration skirt (*feestrok*). Cotton and silk. H. 76 cm, full width 296 cm. Netherlands, 1945–1955. Rijksmuseum, Amsterdam.

Above right:
Vintage postcard. Young girl in the traditional costume of the island of Marken, including a pinafore in floral chintz.

Dresses, jackets, skirts, pinafores, bonnets and headscarves were produced and the baskets of dressmakers filled up with precious and carefully salvaged offcuts. The door was wide open for Dutch quilts to take off.

According to research by An Moonen, author of *A History of Dutch Quilts* (2010), the quilts of the Netherlands were characterized by a variety of chintzes with floral motifs and by compositions primarily made up of pairs of triangles, now often known as 'Dutch triangles', and generally framed by a border.

The quilt shown here, which features the date of its making ('ANNO 1796') embroidered inside the hearts around the central motif, is a perfect example of Dutch patchwork. It is composed of over eight hundred right-angled triangles, paired to form squares. The triangles seem to spin like the sails of a windmill, thanks to the alternation of light and dark shades. It is almost impossible to spot two fabrics that are identical. Imported chintzes are combined with Indian-inspired florals of European origin from the workshops of the Netherlands and Alsace, and even from the Oberkampf factory in Jouy-en-Josas, France. A quilt with an identical design, probably brought to the USA by Dutch emigrants, has been found in Pennsylvania and is now preserved at the International Quilt Museum in Lincoln, Nebraska. It can be seen as proof of the close relationship between the textile traditions of Europe and America.

Patchwork quilt. Cotton prints and embroidery. No backing. Two unfinished corners. 265 × 230 cm. Zaanstreek region, Netherlands, 1796. An Moonen Collection.

THE AMERICAS

The beauty of American quilts is often seen to lie in their functionality. This echoes the principle described by Alexis de Tocqueville in *Democracy in America* (1835), which stated: 'the democratic nations ... will cultivate the arts that serve to render life easy, in preference to those whose object is to adorn it; they will habitually prefer the useful to the beautiful, and they will require that the beautiful should be useful.' Nonetheless, this has not prevented these quilts from being elevated to the status of works of art and displayed in museums.

The practice of patchwork in the USA dates back to the colonial period and has followed the growth of the nation. At every stage of its history – the conquest of the West, the Civil War, the abolition of slavery, the struggle for civil rights – different kinds of quilts have been created, reflecting the contemporary political, social and cultural context at every turn.

With the exception of the examples made by the Amish community, the quilts illustrated here were collected by Charles-Édouard de Broin, and chosen from his collection. As the saying goes, every quilt tells a story, and Géraldine Chouard-Véron, professor of American studies, tells the tales behind these magnificent works, giving pride of place to the cultural significance of this popular artform.

Moving through North, Central and South America, our journey continues in Canada, Mexico, Panama and Peru. In those countries, patchwork has developed its own local characteristics, full of skill and imagination, and reflects the identity of local people who have adopted the technique to personalize their clothing.

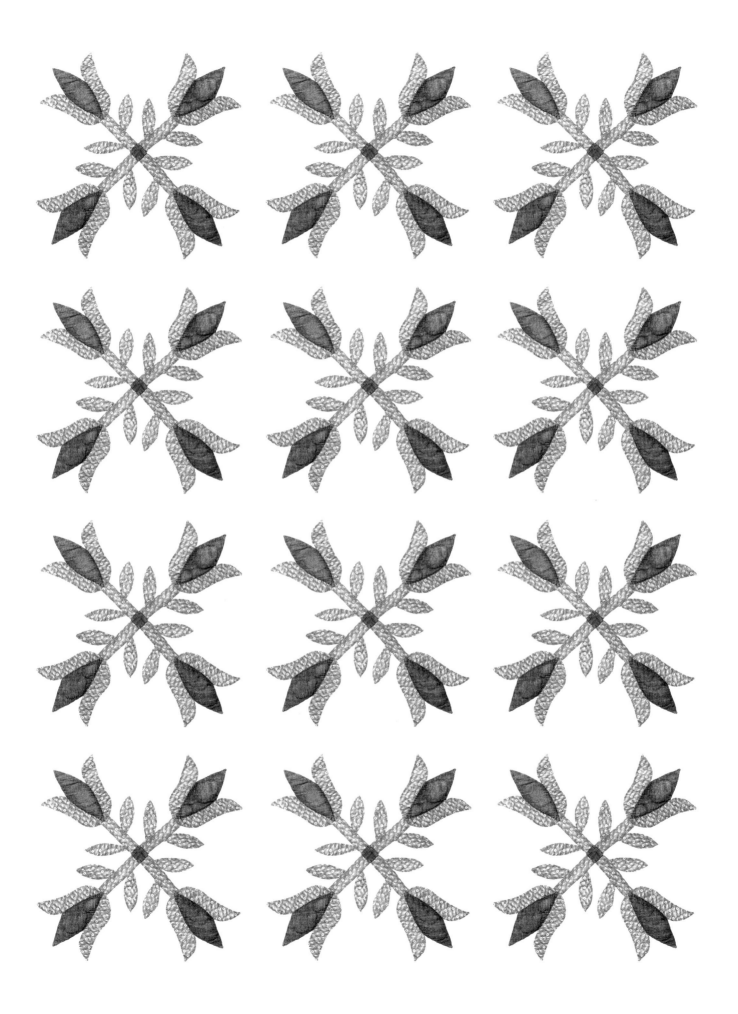

UNITED STATES

LOG CABIN QUILTS

'From log cabin to the White House' is a phrase often used to describe the life of Abraham Lincoln, who was born in a simple log cabin and went on to become President of the United States from 1861 to 1865. In a sense, it's a phrase that encapsulates the American dream.

In the USA, quilting has always been a reflection of the nation. The Log Cabin quilt, inspired by the wooden homes built by early European settlers, particularly those from Scandinavia, is undoubtedly a foundational motif of American patchwork and its many possible design permutations continue to be associated with the USA.

The basic Log Cabin motif consists of rectangular 'logs' laid around a central square; this is often red in colour, to represent hearth and home. By varying the use of light and dark colours, it's possible to create a multitude of different effects. These variant designs have evocative names such as Barn Raising (see right), Furrows, Streak of Lightning, Pinwheels and Courthouse Steps. In a sense, they are a textile recreation of the USA itself, which is built from a patchwork of states.

The Pineapple quilt is another variation of the Log Cabin design. Its rounded, spiky shapes are reminiscent of the pineapple, which is grown in the southern states. Pineapple slices are a traditional accompaniment to the famous Virginia ham; this link may explain the dominance of pinks and reds in many Pineapple quilts.

Above:
Barn Raising Log Cabin quilt. 206 × 208 cm. Mennonite community. Pennsylvania, 1870. Charles-Édouard de Broin Collection.

Opposite, above:
Detail of a Pineapple quilt, a variation on the Log Cabin. 145 × 175 cm. New York, 1890. Catherine Legrand Collection.

Opposite, below:
Detail of a red and white Pineapple quilt. 185 × 225 cm. Georgia, 1890. Charles-Édouard de Broin Collection.

Overleaf, left:
Detail of a Hexagonal Log Cabin quilt. Cotton fabrics, plain, printed or shaped silks. 153 × 163 cm. Connecticut, 1870. Charles-Édouard de Broin Collection.

Overleaf, right:
Detail of a Tumbling Blocks Log Cabin quilt. Cotton and wool fabrics. 168 × 189 cm. Connecticut, 1860–1890. Charles-Édouard de Broin Collection.

BURGOYNE SURROUNDED

Although patchwork quilts have few obvious connections with military history, this design is an exception to the rule. The key to its name lies in the story of America's fight for independence.

At first sight, the simple geometry of the Burgoyne Surrounded quilt (opposite, above) recalls the motifs of jacquard-woven doubleweave coverlets, which were very popular in the mid-19th century. A closer look, however, allows us to make out what looks like a battle plan, rendered in patriotic colours.

Against a blue ground, which might recall the uniforms of soldiers, whose fabric was often recycled for quilts, small white squares form a circular frame around four larger white blocks, grouped together as if defending themselves from attackers. These motifs are connected by a network of lines made up of the same small white squares. They symbolize the American insurgents fighting against the forces of the British Crown during the Revolutionary War.

More specifically, the Burgoyne Surrounded design represents the Battle of Saratoga, which marked a failed British attempt to gain control of the Hudson Valley. The reckless General John Burgoyne was trapped by the numerically superior American forces and was forced to surrender on 17 October 1777, marking the first significant victory of the Revolutionary War.

By around 1860, the same motif was known as the Wheel of Fortune, and incorporated colours other than red, white and blue. Several examples are included in the collections of the Metropolitan Museum of Art, New York.

Opposite above:
Detail of a Burgoyne Surrounded quilt. 190 × 241 cm. Ohio, 1910–1920. Charles-Édouard de Broin Collection.

Opposite below:
Detail of a Drunkard's Path quilt. 188 × 220 cm. New York, 1895. Charles-Édouard de Broin Collection.

DRUNKARD'S PATH

During the 19th century, the practice of quilting moved beyond the home and began to take on an ideological role. Quilting parties became opportunities for American women to engage in forms of political and social expression.

It was at this time that the traditions of the fundraising quilt and the protest quilt were established. Sewn collectively by groups of women, these works were sold at auction to benefit various causes. The Women's Christian Temperance Union (WCTU) was formed in 1873 in Ohio to combat alcoholism in men which was rampant after the Civil War. Many WCTU quilts used the Drunkard's Path design, a zigzag pattern that recalls a trail of staggering footsteps. Like many American quilts, it was inspired by existing quilt blocks such as Solomon's Path, Old Maid's Puzzle or Mill Wheel, and adapted to suit the needs of the abstinence movement. The combination of white, symbolizing the purity of water, with blue or red, the colours of the WCTU, made it a patriotic piece that was fit to promote a healthier nation.

The distinguishing feature of this design is the sewing of curved pieces, which is a tricky operation. The basic block is a quarter circle placed in the corner of a square; sixteen blocks are then combined, mixing convex and concave curves to create a larger block with a distinctive twisting 'path'. The overall visual impact is striking, especially on larger quilts, and was therefore well suited to public display before an auction. The meticulous nature of the work can also be seen in the impressive quilting, which uses small, close stitches – the very antithesis of the staggering drunkard's steps. The design is also notable for its longevity, as these quilts continued to be made until Prohibition arrived in the 1920s.

SAMPLER QUILT

This charming quilt may bring to mind
***The Little House on the Prairie* (1932–1943),**
an autobiographical series of books
by Laura Ingalls Wilder, based on her
childhood in an American pioneer family in
the late 19th century. In the 1970s, the TV
series based on the books led to a revival
in the popularity of patchwork quilts.

Sampler quilts were inspired by embroidery
samplers, usually embroidered in cross stitch,
which were popular in the 19th century. The
embroiderer's name and the date are usually
included, alongside a wholesome motto
such as 'Home sweet home'. The sewing of a
sampler was a rite of passage for many young
American girls. Among the features inherited
from its embroidered cousin, this patchwork
quilt includes the signature of the quilter
embroidered in blue lettering in the centre.

    Made in 1890 by a woman named Mary
Swank, the quilt was probably made with
the help of female friends or family. Typical
of the folk art of its day, it is a spontaneous
expression of the joy of having one's own
home and wanting for nothing.

    The central panel is a Little House motif,
flanked by two flowering branches, not to
scale. A sunflower takes the place of the sun,
while a hand motif adds a striking personal
touch to the composition. It is possible to
recognize around fifty different quilt motifs,
Some are common – Nine Patch, Jacob's
Ladder – while others are less so, including
Basket, Bow Ties and Carolina Lily. The regular
inclusion of chequerboard squares gives a
structure to the whole design. It is interesting
to compare this design with the album quilt,
another style of quilt that combined multiple
motifs into a single design.

Sampler quilt. 166 × 200 cm.
Pennsylvania, 1890. Charles-
Édouard de Broin Collection.

HAWAIIAN STAR QUILTS

The quilts of Polynesia are characterized by their intricate appliqué motifs that form a radiating medallion, hence the name of Hawaiian Star. In Tahiti, this style of quilt is known as a *tifaifai*, from the word *tifai*, meaning 'to patch up' or 'to mend'. Popular plant motifs include the ulu leaf, which comes from the breadfruit tree, and the bird-of-paradise flower.

In the late 18th and early 19th centuries, the wives of Protestant missionaries taught sewing techniques to the people of Polynesia. At a time when woven fabric was a rare commodity, Polynesian women adopted patchwork as a way of recycling older textiles, and then began to use it to make colourful creations inspired by the local flora. This style soon became popular throughout the Pacific Islands.

The technique is fairly straightforward. First, a square of plain fabric is folded into four or eight. Using a paper template, a pattern is drawn on a quarter or eighth of the fabric, then carefully cut out along the lines. When the fabric is unfolded, a radiating symmetrical motif is created. This is tacked onto a white ground and then sewn in place. The quilting stitches are arranged in concentric waves, following the outline of the motifs.

This style of design was inspired by the art of paper cutting, which was a popular pastime in the 18th century. It also recalls the art of Matisse, who loved 'cutting into colour' to create collages. His trip to Tahiti in 1930 inspired his painting *Souvenir d'Océanie*, as well as a set of liturgical robes decorated with stars and appliquéd flowers, which he designed for a chapel in Vence (see p. 202).

The two-tone quilt shown opposite dates from 1910–1920, shortly after the annexation of Hawaii by the United States in 1898. It could be considered a cousin of the Carolina Lily (see p. 67), a popular design during the same period. It is sewn in appliqué and carefully quilted. The small motifs are simpler versions of the larger Hawaiian Star, and are likewise obtained by folding and cutting the fabric. Framed like a painting, it marks a time when quilts were no longer considered merely functional household items, and could be hung on a wall simply as decoration.

Above, from top to bottom:
Hawaiian Star quilt. Appliqué and quilting. 213 × 239 cm. Hawaii, 1900–1972. American Museum, Bath.

Queen Kapi'olani's Fan Quilt. Appliqué and quilting. 191 × 221 cm. Hawaii, 1900–1924. American Museum, Bath.

Opposite:
Hawaiian Star quilt detail. Appliqué and quilting. 176 × 200 cm. Hawaii, 1910–1920. Charles-Édouard de Broin Collection.

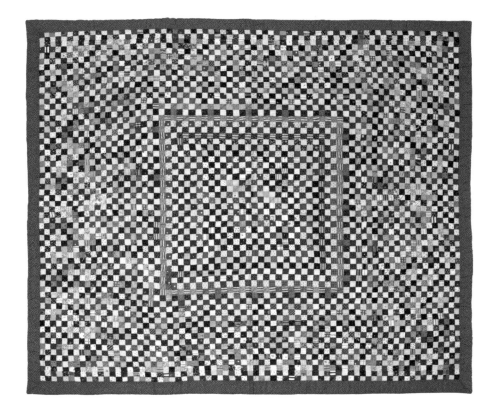

POSTAGE STAMP QUILTS

**Patchwork has always been a thrifty
artform: any remnants left over from
making clothing or domestic items were
kept in stash bags and eventually recycled
into quilts. Made up of thousands of
squares no bigger than postage stamps,
this quilt is a wonderful example of this.**

Present since colonial times and throughout
the 19th century and embodying the Puritan
sense of frugality, postage stamp quilts were
popular in times of crisis, particularly during
the Great Depression.

Although simple in appearance, this
bedspread is unusual. Its skilful composition
becomes apparent with close observation.
A block of dark colours, beiges and browns,
sixteen squares by sixteen, stands in the
centre like a medallion. It is surrounded by a
series of square borders, each with a different
colour scheme. The regularity of this central
area contrasts with the deliberately disorderly
array of colours that make up the rest of the
quilt. The quilters were clearly both patient and
painstaking to arrange and sew so many tiny
squares. The finished piece is lightly quilted
on the diagonal.

This quilt is striking for the variety of fabrics
it contains. In fact, it is virtually a catalogue of
textiles of the 1840s: patterned cottons, florals,
checks, geometrics, plains and semi-plains.
An understanding of fabrics is a vital skill
when dating a quilt; it was for this reason that
Barbara Brackman, an expert in the history of
American quilts, published *Clues in the Calico*
(1989), which became an invaluable reference
book in the field, listing all the clues necessary
to identify a particular design.

As a popular artform, quilts have regularly
been featured on real-life US postage
stamps. These are particularly admired by
stamp collectors, quilters, and anyone who
appreciates the beauty of patchwork, even
when reduced down to stamp size.

YO-YO QUILT

The fabrics of vintage yo-yo quilts reflect their era, the 1930s and 1940s. Made from boldly coloured or floral cottons taken from old summer dresses or grandmas' aprons, these quilts were a way of dealing with the restrictions of the Great Depression.

Americans call this a yo-yo quilt, but in Britain, the style is known as Suffolk puffs, from the name of the county southeast of London. Sources date its origin to around 1600, and it is said that tufts of wool from Suffolk sheep were once used to stuff the individual puffs.

The first step is to cut out circles of fabric, with a diameter that rarely exceeds a few inches. This economical technique requires little more than small scraps of silk or cotton and an upside-down bowl or saucer to use as a template. Once the circles have been cut, a gathering thread is sewn close to the edge of each circle. It is pulled tight to gather the fabric, and then knotted to fix it in place. Just like that, the first yo-yo is complete.

The overall effect depends on the choice of fabrics, which are sorted according to style, colour and size, and on the way they are arranged. The yo-yos can be scattered at random to achieve a *millefiori* effect, or arranged in fours, nines or sixteens of the same colour to create a tessellated design. Diamonds, hexagons, triangles, rectangles, stripes or concentric squares can all be utilized to produce a mosaic effect. Other potential variations include overlapping the yo-yos instead of arranging them side by side, mixing yo-yos of different sizes, or slipping cotton wool or batting inside to make them padded.

Most yo-yo quilts date from the first half of the 20th century, but the late 19th century saw the rise of a similar style made up of squares of padded fabric, known as a puff quilt, bubble quilt or biscuit quilt.

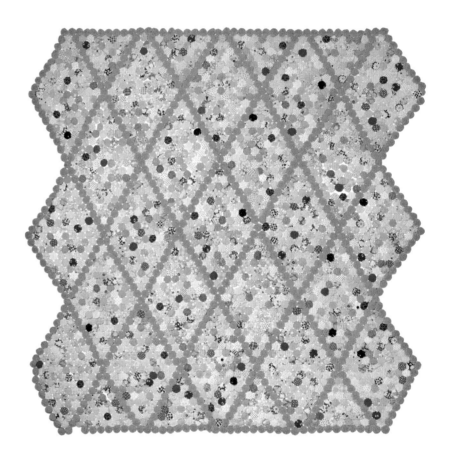

Above and opposite (detail): Yo-yo quilt, made of approx. 2,500 circles cut from printed and plain cottons. 200 × 200 cm. USA. Lena Bibring Collection.

CAROLINA LILY
& POMEGRANATE QUILTS

Every state in the US has its own official flower. The magnolia represents Mississippi, the iris Tennessee, and the sunflower Kansas. These emblems feature prominently in the textile arts. There is even a design called the 50 State Flowers quilt, which includes the full set.

Flowers have inspired a great many quilts, including the Carolina Lily, one of the most popular patterns of the 19th century, to the extent of its becoming an emblematic motif of this period, well beyond the Southern states. The Carolina Lily quilt shown above is striking for its balanced composition. A green garland adorned with fanciful flowers and small red birds frames a dozen posies made from four crossed lilies, forming a design that recalls the gardens of the Deep South. The technique of appliqué is well suited to this type of motif. The centres of the lilies are lightly padded, the quilting is elaborate. A network of curves

and scrolling lines adds a sense of rhythm to the bucolic design.

The Pomegranate quilt, dating from the same period, is similar to the Carolina Lily in its colours and in the symmetry of the composition. As a symbol of fertility, the pomegranate, also known as the 'candy apple' motif, was often used for wedding quilts. The quilt shown opposite is notable for the skilful appliqué work used to create the pomegranates, combining bright green leaves with the red fruits, cut from a Persian-influenced cotton print.

Because of their festive colours, these quilts were often displayed during the Christmas period. These are two perfect examples of American quilters creating elegant designs based on nature. When an appliqué pattern became popular, quilters often reproduced it using traditional piecing techniques, which gave these designs additional longevity.

Above:
Carolina Lily quilt. Appliqué and quilting. 180 × 215 cm. Pennsylvania, 1830–1850. Charles-Édouard de Broin Collection.

Opposite:
Pomegranate quilt (detail). Appliqué and quilting. 208 × 212 cm. Maryland, 1840. Charles-Édouard de Broin Collection.

CIGAR RIBBON QUILTS

In 19th-century New York, high society men would often gather in the library after dinner to smoke a cigar, while the women continued their conversation in the living room. At least, that is how these soirées were described by Edith Wharton in novels such as *The Age of Innocence* (1920).

At that time, cigars were sold in cedar boxes containing bundles of ten to fifty cigars, tied with a yellow silk ribbon that bore the maker's mark. Evocative brand names such as Senators, Grand Master and White Sailor appealed to image-conscious gentlemen, while Spanish labels such as La Natividad, Romeo y Julieta and Havana Imperial were also highly coveted. The first cigar factory in New York opened in 1870.

Accustomed to the art of recycling, women began to save the silk ribbons that wrapped the cigars and incorporated them into crazy quilts (see p. 70), adding a vivid flash of yellow to the velvets and satins. The two quilts shown here are striking because they are made from nothing but cigar ribbons, arranged in patterns that make fine use of the different shades of silk, the black and red lettering, and even the length of the manufacturers' names, stacking them into pyramid-shaped blocks. While very different from traditional Log Cabin quilts (see p. 52), these quilts nevertheless echo those motifs due to their combination of square blocks and log-like bands.

Ideas for textile projects were often printed in mass-market women's magazines and these two quilts may well have been inspired by just such a source. Between 1875 and 1910, publications such as *Good Housekeeping* and *Ladies' Home Journal* published designs for cushions or tablecloths that their readers could make by recycling silk cigar ribbons.

In a similar spirit but in another era and a different sociocultural context, we find feed sack quilts. During the Great Depression of the 1930s, women began to make quilts from the canvas bags in which flour and animal feed were sold. To bolster this craft, the manufacturers printed colourful motifs on their sacks that could be easily incorporated into quilts. This is another fine example of the endless creativity of American quilters.

Above:
Quilt made from silk cigar ribbons. 80 × 154 cm. New York, 1910. Charles-Édouard de Broin Collection.

Opposite:
Quilt made from silk cigar ribbons (detail). Herringbone stitch embroidery. Fringed border made from folded cigar ribbons. 80 × 80 cm. New York, 1910. Charles-Édouard de Broin Collection.

CRAZY QUILTS

Patchwork is not always staid and orderly – far from it. In 1876, during the World's Fair in Philadelphia celebrating the centenary of American Independence, visitors were enraptured by the decorative arts of Japan, including crazed porcelain and coloured silks, which immediately became a new source of inspiration for the popular arts and for patchwork in particular. The result was a bold style of patchwork made from irregular pieces – the crazy quilt.

With its imaginative patterns, promoted in contemporary women's magazines of the time and quickly embraced by keen quilters, the crazy quilt offered liberation from the shackles of strict geometry. It was a world in which pieces of fabric of all sizes, patterns and sources could be placed side by side, with no rules to follow. The crazy quilt provided an opportunity for quilters to promote their own heritage as well as their skill. Velvets and silks mingled with taffetas, satins and brocades in compositions overflowing with ribbons and braids, embroidered with herringbone stitch, feather stitch and more. The quilt on the right is edged with a scalloped border of black velvet teardrops and incorporates scraps of luxurious fabrics, deployed with great creativity. It also features symbols of good luck that were typical of the crazy patchwork style, like the horseshoe, the pansy, the star and the heart.

The quilt shown opposite, made by a book club, can be deciphered like a puzzle. Dated 1898, this rather rustic crazy quilt is a collective work that tells a charming story: that of Becky, Amy, Jill, Emma and other women who are only recorded by their initials. As founder members of a book club, the Easton Literary Ladies (stitched in full at the bottom of the quilt), they created a design inspired by the books they had read. While a house, a horse and a boot might conjure up a rural tale, and a snowman seems to be taken from a Christmas story, a sailing boat and a red hot air balloon act as an invitation to adventure. A curved row of coloured bands forms a rough version of a fan, a recurring motif in crazy quilts. Embroidered details include a spider's web – a symbol of patience – and a pair of scissors, harking back to the time of the quilt's creation. Another touching detail is a tiny patchwork of black and white fabric, almost a quilt within a quilt.

The crazy quilt had its heyday at around the same time that it first became respectable to display a quilt hung on a wall, like a work of art. However, the flamboyant fashion for crazy patchwork only lasted a few decades and fell from popularity in around 1910.

Below:
Crazy quilt. Cotton, silk, velvet, embroidery. 175 × 175 cm. New York, c. 1880. Charles-Édouard de Broin Collection.

Opposite:
Crazy quilt made by the Easton Literary Ladies (detail). Cotton, silk, velvet, wool, synthetic fabric. Embroidery stitches. 100 × 116 cm. Pennsylvania, 1898. Charles-Édouard de Broin Collection.

Opposite:
Sixteen Patch quilt.
Woollen fabrics. Mutual aid
quilt made by Malinda Blank.
198 × 197 cm. 2005.

*Above, from left to right
and top to bottom:*
Sunshine & Shadow quilt.
Woollen cambric. Wedding
quilt made by Annie Stoltzfus.
207 × 207 cm. 1950.

Sunshine & Shadow quilt.
Woollen cambric. Wedding
quilt made by Melinda
Stoltzfus. 190 × 190 cm. 1945.

Double Nine Patch quilt.
Woollen cambric. Wedding
quilt made by Elsie Kings.
205 × 205 cm. 1951.

Centre Diamond quilt.
Woollen cambric. Mutual aid
quilt made by Barbara Fisher.
214 × 214 cm. 1957.

All quilts: Pennsylvania.
Jacques Légeret Collection.

AMISH QUILTS

The Amish principle of *Gelassenheit* is based on a German word meaning 'yielding to authority'. To explain its meaning, it seems appropriate to turn to Jacques Légeret, the collector of these quilts, who has spent a great deal of time with the Amish communities of Pennsylvania and Indiana: 'The term implies modesty, the rejection of competition, the acceptance of the vagaries of life, in short, a way of living'. If *Gelassenheit* is the essence of Amish life, the *Ordnung*, a set of written and oral rules set out in the 16th century, is its driving force. Interpreting an Amish quilt therefore requires a comprehension of the 'driving force' and the 'essence' of the lives of those who made it.

The Amish did not invent the art of quilting. They discovered it through contact with rural American women towards the end of the 19th century, and found the craft to be well suited to their frugality, their modesty and the moral obligation not to waste anything. Even today, Amish women make all their family's clothes, and scraps of fabric, old or new, might be preserved for years. One rule prevails: all the fabrics must be plain – prints are prohibited, as they are considered too frivolous. Seated at a wooden quilting frame, Amish women come up with endless combinations of squares, triangles, rhomboids and rectangles, using all the colours of the rainbow. Depending on the community, the fabrics used are cotton and wool, and sometimes Dacron for tourists.

The three best-known Amish quilt designs are the Centre Diamond, Bars, and Sunshine & Shadow. The Centre Diamond deviates from the usual rules of patchwork, since it requires large pieces of fabric, which must usually be specially bought. It was popular as a wedding quilt from the 1910s to 1950s in Pennsylvania, a period of relative prosperity for those communities. In other states, especially Ohio and Indiana, Amish women expressed their imaginations by creating different arrangements of smaller geometric shapes.

Understanding an Amish quilt is simple: it is above all an act of love. Women make them to mark three important events in their lives: birth, marriage and mutual aid. So-called 'mutual aid' quilts are frequently auctioned off to help a member of the community with medical or other expenses. Now admired by the wider world as works of art, Amish quilts nevertheless remain a cultural touchstone that reflects the importance of *Gelassenheit*.

AFRICAN AMERICAN QUILTS

'Kneeling in the keeping room where [Sethe] usually went to talk-think it was clear why Baby Suggs was so starved for color. There wasn't any except for two orange squares in a quilt that made the absence shout...'

Beloved, Toni Morrison's 1988 Pulitzer-winning novel, recounts the story of a formerly enslaved woman who was driven to kill her own daughter in order to save her from a life of servitude. This dark tale, which begins in the 1870s, after the Civil War, opens with the image of a threadbare bedspread, inviting a reading that gives the quilt symbolic resonance.

The quilt shown here dates from the 1940s, when racial segregation in the USA was still in force in the Southern states. Originating from the state of Virginia, it is characterized by the intense colours of its unpatterned fabrics and the lively rhythm that defines the style of African American quilts. Made with low-cost fabrics, mostly synthetics, the composition is inspired by the Log Cabin design (see p. 52), but simplified to include only four logs around each square, which vary in size.

In many respects, this quilt recalls those made by the women of Gee's Bend, Alabama, a rural community established by former enslaved people, whose bold and imaginative creations have received a great deal of attention in recent years, including becoming the subject of an article in the *New York Times* in 2021. Gee's Bend quilts now hang on the walls of the greatest American museums, and constitute an important chapter in the story of American quilting and African American art.

Detail of an African American quilt. Synthetic fabrics. 180 × 214 cm. Virginia, 1940. Charles-Édouard de Broin Collection.

Below:
Seminole skirt. Plain cotton.
H. 67 cm, full width 200 cm.
Big Cypress Reservation,
Florida, 1930–1940.
Ah-Tah-Thi-Ki Museum,
Clewiston, Florida.

Above:
Vintage postcard. A Seminole chief with his family, 1930s.

SEMINOLE GARMENTS

On the postcard above, dating from the 1930s, Chief Sam Willis and other members of his family are pictured outside a Miccosukee house in Tropical Hobbyland, a tourist village in the Florida Everglades.

The Seminole and Miccosukee people of today are descended from a diverse group of Native Americans in the southeastern USA who cohabited with British, Spanish and French colonizers in the fertile lands of Georgia and Alabama. In the early 1700s, under pressure from English settlers, they were forced to settle in Florida, then owned by the Spanish Crown, where they integrated with other indigenous peoples of south and central Florida.

In 1819, when the USA purchased Florida from Spain, the Seminole lands were again much coveted and the Treaty of Moultrie Creek caused further displacement. Some Seminole people were forced to emigrate and settle on reservations in Oklahoma. Those who resisted spent years in conflict with the authorities. Eventually, the last Seminoles, without ever having signed a treaty, took

refuge in the Everglades and it was not until 1891 that land was officially assigned to them.

The postcard shows the chief's wife and her daughters-in-law dressed in gathered ponchos and full skirts made from strips of patchwork alternating with plain stripes. The chief himself is wearing a shirt of patchwork bands. Native American patchwork has its roots in the late 19th century, when Native settlements first acquired hand-cranked Singer sewing machines, later followed by pedal-powered and electric versions. Some missionary women gave sewing lessons, and an abundance of cotton fabrics from the textile industries of the North were available, and could be bought or bartered at trading posts.

Seminole patchwork, in which the pieces can be measured in fractions of an inch, is captivating in its detail. Behind the intricate stitching lies a clever technique. Rather than using a combination of blocks or triangles, the fabric is carefully cut into narrow bands. The colours are selected and the bands are arranged into groups of three or five, and sewn together to create a long block composed of thin stripes. This block is then cut into short vertical strips of equal width, which are rearranged diagonally at a 45-degree angle. These pieces are then stitched together to create a band with a stepped motif. There are hundreds of possible variations on this basic technique, bearing names such as Cross, Sacred Fire, Broken Arrow, Man on Horseback, Lightning, and Diamondback Rattlesnake.

Right:
Strip of Seminole patchwork. Cotton. 240 × 6 cm. Florida, c. 1950. Elisabeth Gratacap Collection.

CANADA

POINTES FOLLES

The maple trees are aflame, autumn has arrived on Île d'Orléans, bathed by the St Lawrence River, a little downstream from Quebec City. Quilts and bedspreads, hung across the railings, are being aired out one last time before winter comes.

Retailles (trimmings) are what Quebecois quilters call the scraps of fabric and remnants from old clothes that they recycle into patchwork. A piece torn from a jacket might sit next to a strip from a worn-out trouser leg or a remnant from the skirt of a tweed suit. Twill, felt, brushed cloth, façonné, *cheviotte*, crushed velvet, flannelette: the combination of fabrics gives this heavy quilt an old-fashioned look.

Pointes folles ('crazy stitches') is the Quebecois term for a crazy quilt (see p. 70). The irregular pieces are held together by all sorts of embroidery stitches: French knots, chain stitch, feather stitch, couching and stem stitch. The one shown opposite may well have been created by many hands at a *cercle de fermières*, a sort of club where Canadian women living in rural areas could come together. The *cercle* provided an opportunity to sew together, quilting a finished bedcover by stitching through the layers with a cord.

This crazy quilt is relatively restrained, with a simple yellow feather stitch used throughout to cover the seams. Its twenty blocks, each measuring around 40 cm square, are arranged in five rows. The scraps of red woollen fabric scattered across the composition enliven the palette of muted colours. Each block also includes a piece of yellow velvet, giving a rhythm to the composition. In Log Cabin quilts from USA (see p. 52), the colour red in the centre of each block is said to symbolize the warmth of a hearth. Here, it is perhaps the last rays of Quebec autumn sunshine that illuminate the work.

Opposite:
Pointes folles quilt (detail). Used woollen fabrics. Embroidery. 210 × 170 cm. Quebec, c. 1950. Catherine Legrand Collection.

Left:
Stash of fabric offcuts, known in Quebecois French as *retailles*. Tuulikki Chompré Collection.

MEXICO

MAYA SKIRT AND APRON

Many indigenous Mexican garments were radically changed by the arrival of the Spanish colonists, but the traditional Maya skirt, known as a *falda*, *morga* or *corte*, remains almost unchanged. The skirt is a simple tube made from around 3 metres of fabric, which the wearer wraps around her waist, folding it at the front and holding it in place with a braided belt.

Mass-produced ribbons and lace are very popular in Mexico and can often be seen on indigenous clothing, including the *huipils* (blouses) of the Nahua people or the Zapotecs of the Oaxaca region. As well as being stitched to clothing, ribbons are also braided together and woven into women's hair, or used to adorn the hats of Chamula or Zinacantán men.

In the covered market in Ocasingo, the seamstresses can be seen hard at work. Long lengths of ribbon scroll under the presser foot of their sewing machines, unwinding from bobbins placed in a basket on the ground. The ribbons (*listones*) are sewn edge to edge or slightly spaced, forming a rainbow around the middle of the skirt. Nowadays, black mass-produced cotton often replaces the traditional indigo-dyed cotton weave. The patchwork decoration is fairly simple, requiring only straight lines of stitching, but sewing a synthetic ribbon is not straightforward – it wrinkles easily, so care must be taken to keep the tension even.

These braid-trimmed skirts serve as markers of cultural identity; a Tzeltal woman from Abasolo or Ocosingo will never be mistaken for anyone else. However, fashions change in Chiapas just as they do in Paris or Tokyo, and any new innovation will be quickly seized upon and imitated. The current popularity of glossy synthetic ribbons in bold colours, sometimes embellished with golden edges, is simply the latest example of this. Far from being frozen in time, indigenous costumes are constantly changing, and museums and collectors must work hard to record each new development.

While the Maya skirt has pre-Columbian roots, the apron shown opposite, with its ruffles, pockets and bib, has clear Hispanic origins. Popular in both Mexico and Guatemala, indigenous aprons feature a spectacular range of pleats, frills and gathers that combine to create a truly dazzling effect.

Opposite:
An apron (*delantal*) worn by a young Tzeltal girl. Synthetic materials. Ocosingo, Mexico.

Right:
A Tzeltal woman wearing a traditional skirt (*falda*). Indigo-dyed cotton with appliqué decoration of multicoloured synthetic ribbons. Ocosingo, Mexico.

PANAMA

MOLA

The small islands of the Guna archipelago can only be reached by plane and canoe. They resemble huge sea turtles, studded with rows of palm-roofed huts. Only about forty islands are inhabited out of the approximately three hundred and sixty that make up the San Blas Islands, a territory with partially autonomous status located off the Caribbean coast of Panama.

204-San Blas Indian Women

This string of islands is the home of the *mola*, a work of textile art that is used to decorated the blouses of indigenous women and has earned the archipelago a worldwide reputation.

The *mola* is a rectangular piece of fabric measuring about 30 by 40 cm. *Molas* are made in pairs, with one being worn on the front of a blouse and the other on the back, with the maker generally preferring to reserve the finest one for the back. The *mola* is made using the technique of reverse appliqué, a craft shared by several other communities around the world. The women of the Hmong communities in Laos and Vietnam and the Miao people of China use a very similar technique to decorate collars, belts, bags or baby carriers (see pp. 172 and 176–179), while the Banjara community in India and the people of Sind also decorate textiles in this way (see pp. 130 and 138).

To make a *mola*, several layers of fabric are laid on top of each other and tacked together. A design is sketched on the topmost layer. The seamstress then cuts through the top layer of fabric to reveal the colour of the fabric below. Using the end of her needle to turn the edge under, the seamstress hems the cut fabric, and begins to build up a design. The materials required are simple: plain cotton fabrics, spools of thread, a fine needle, a pair of sharp scissors. Nothing is wasted; the scraps cut from one *mola* will be used for the next.

In general, the more layers there are, and the more colours, the more beautiful the design is considered to be. In practice, this is not always the case, as there are some very lovely two-tone *molas*, but the current fashion favours as many colours as possible. In addition to the two or three base layers, the seamstress sometimes slips in small pieces in an additional colour to add detail, and completes her work with embroidery stitches.

Motifs may spring from anywhere. Some *molas* are inspired by nature: a coral reef, a palm leaf; or local fauna: a sea urchin, a hermit crab, a ray, two pelicans, a sea turtle, four monkeys. Others depict everyday objects: a canoe, a paddle, a gourd, fish hooks. Still others draw on more abstract concepts: a storm, the moon, whirlwinds, disease, or take inspiration from pop culture, featuring figures such as Santa Claus or cartoon characters.

The *mola* is very much a living artform, but this fact also makes it vulnerable. Influenced by tourist demand, seamstresses often favour figurative motifs that will sell easily, rather than older geometric designs. To make money, they must save on time and fabric, so will limit the number of layers and may sew on additional

Left:
Vintage postcard showing Guna women. The image shows how the length of the blouse and the size of the *mola* have decreased over time.

Opposite, below:
Two *molas* with 2 or 3 layers. Cotton and synthetics. Approx. 50 × 30 cm. Panama. Liliane and Armel Chichery Collection.

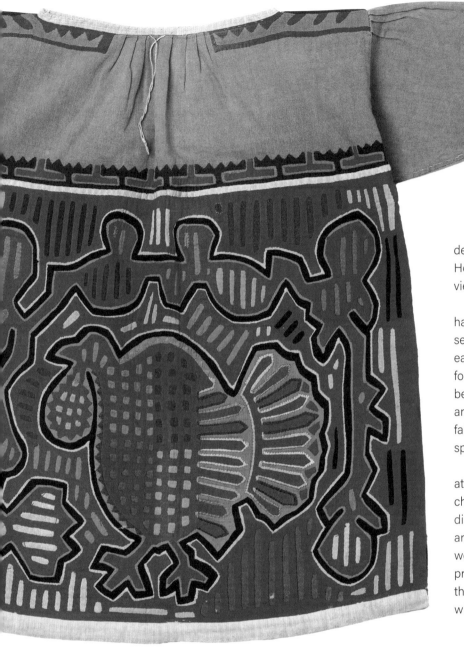

Left:
Guna blouse with *mola*. Cotton fabric. 61 × 55 cm, arm span 83 cm. Comarca de San Blas, Panama, c. 1950. Tuulikki Chompré Collection.

Overleaf:
Guna blouse with *mola*. 2 layers and additional colours. Cotton fabrics. Appliqué and reverse appliqué. 51 × 32 cm. Catherine Legrand Collection.

details instead of using reverse appliqué. However, these modifications can also be viewed positively, as signs of vitality in the art.

Through the making of *molas*, Guna women have succeeded in combining the pleasure of sewing and creating with the satisfaction of earning an income and gaining recognition for their work. Paid for in dollars, *molas* can become a source of financial independence and the profits can pay for everything from fabrics and needles to sewing machines and spectacles when required.

A minority people, the Guna are seriously at risk from rising sea levels linked to climate change. Their islands are in danger of disappearing forever, taking their traditions and skills with them. However, the Guna are well aware of these challenges and fight proudly to protect their islands, their language, their cultural identity and their textile traditions, with remarkable energy and resilience.

PERU

MONTERA

Here is another example of clothing as a marker of cultural identity. The traditional hats worn by the Quechua people in the regions of Cuzco, Chinchero and neighbouring villages are striking objects.

The name *montera* is potentially confusing. On one hand, it is a general term used to describe a cloth hat, but on the other hand, the word is most closely associated with the black astrakhan hats traditionally worn in the bullfighting arena. In this case, however, it refers simply to the hats worn by women going about their daily business at the local market.

This flat-topped hat is worn by both married women and men. Its decoration, size and colour scheme may vary slightly from one village to another but the basic construction is always the same: a stiff ring about 30 cm in diameter, a slightly convex dish shape is formed from plaited plant fibres, with a central hole beneath to fit on the head. A chin strap keeps the hat in place. This hat offers protection from sun and rain. Its framework is hidden beneath pieces of red and black woollen fabric, with added touches of yellow and green, which are felted naturally by the humid climate. The coloured pieces are stitched down with visible seams.

In Chinchero, a border of red woollen petals runs around the edge of the hat; elsewhere, this is replaced by a simple braid. Each village has its own style of decoration: simple stitched-on fabric shapes, ribbons, appliqué braids, sequins and spangles, embroidered motifs. Fresh flowers may even be added. But whatever the decoration, care is always taken to respect the hat's primary function as a marker of cultural identity.

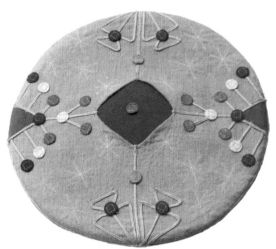

Above:
Traditional hats. Plant fibre, woollen fabric, braids, glass beads, embroidery. Diameter: 25 to 30 cm. From villages in the area around Cuzco, Peru. Lilian and Armel Chichery Collection.

Opposite:
Woman wearing a *montera*. Chinchero, Peru.

APPLIQUÉ FROM SANTO TOMÁS

When a Quechua woman bends down to pick up her belongings, the beauty of her layered skirts and white petticoats is revealed, unfurling like the petals of a flower. Each layer is edged with braid or a band of embroidery or appliqué decoration. The gathered skirt (*falda*), jacket (*jaqueta*) and hat (*montera*) are based on the Spanish costumes worn during the colonial period.

The village of Santo Tomás, about an eight-hour drive from Cuzco, is situated more than 3,500 metres above sea level, in the province of Chumbivilcas. In these isolated mountains, horses are a vital form of transport, and Quechua women wear heeled boots, short fitted jackets and wide skirts that are suitable for regular riding. Each village has its own style, which is how women recognize each other when they meet at market.

The women of Santo Tomás (see opposite) traditionally wear a black woollen skirt adorned with a broad band of red velvet, decorated with cut-out motifs. The velvet is not made locally, so must be bought or bartered for. Matching appliqué decoration adorns the collar, cuffs, lapels and bottom edge of their jackets. Their felt hats are manufactured locally.

The jacket is made from black and white wool serge, woven on a treadle loom with a chevron or diamond motif. The basic skirt is unpatterned, in brown or black wool. A scalloped red braid forms the lowest band of decoration. Then comes a broad band of velvet, about 30 cm wide, running all the way around the skirt. The cuts and incisions are made with a pair of sharp scissors using a template. The floral motifs, usually large petals or leaves, fit together but do not necessarily repeat. They are very similar to the patterns of the Yi tunic (see pages 202–203). Cutting

out the motifs and then turning the edges of the soft velvet is a delicate operation. Velvet is a woven fabric with a layer of cut pile, which gives softness but also makes the fabric fragile. Nilda Callañaupa Alvarez, who has documented the traditions of Santo Tomás in detail, explains that this painstaking appliqué work is often done by a seamstress who makes the *jaquetas* and *faldas* in her shop with fabric brought to her by the weavers.

Opposite:
The weaver Susana Huamini Gonzales wearing the traditional hat, jacket and skirt of the village of Santo Tomás. Woven wool and cut velvet appliqué. Province of Chumbivilcas, Peru.

Right:
Layers of skirts decorated with appliqué and embroidery around the hem. Pisac market, Cuzco region, Peru.

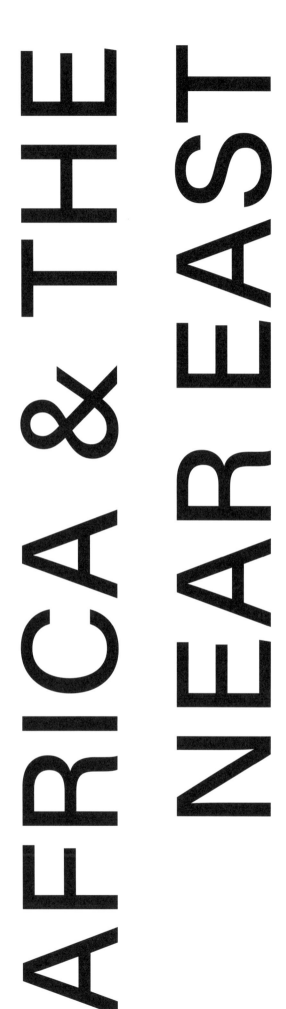

AFRICA & THE NEAR EAST

In West Africa, from Senegal to Cameroon, the narrow width of traditional looms means that any length of non-industrially made fabric tends to be made up of a series of strips. Nonetheless, these textiles are not usually considered patchwork. The most uniquely African form of patchwork is probably to be found on Kuba cloths, made from beaten bark or raffia. Elsewhere, the practice of patchwork is often a reappropriation by local artisans of skills imported by colonialism, a form of reinterpretation that has created distinct markers of cultural identity. While economic constraints are regularly a factor in the use of patchwork and appliqué, aesthetic and cultural considerations are frequently the driving force here. Traditional textiles are a time-honoured way of displaying affiliation to a group. Another distinctive feature of African patchwork is that it is often men who perform the jobs of cutting, stitching, assembling and embroidering, whether by hand or with a sewing machine.

The Middle East is a region that has long been famed for its textiles. The ancient Coptic peoples decorated their tunics with inlaid or appliqué strips and medallions. The standards that served as rallying points for the Saracen armies fighting the Crusaders were richly decorated with appliqué and embroidery. Christian chroniclers also noted the magnificence of the Saracens' military tents, canopies and horse regalia. But throughout the history of these lands, men and women, in urban and rural environments, wove, dyed, sewed and embroidered. Although many workshops have now disappeared due to conflict and political turmoil, textile traditions are still being kept alive by a few resilient communities.

NAMIBIA

HERERO 'LONG' DRESS

'Why would the Herero adopt the clothes of the very people who cost them so dearly?' asks photographer Jim Naughten in *Conflict and Costumes* (2013), a book that showcases Naughten's portraits of Herero women dressed in magnificent full-length gowns and Herero men wearing the uniforms of their former colonizers.

The Herero people of Namibia belong to the Bantu ethnic group. In 1904, the Herero rose up against the German colonists who were occupying their land. The revolt was brutally suppressed by General Lothar von Trotha, and ended in a bloodbath. Nearly 80% of the Herero population was murdered and the survivors were placed in work camps, a sinister foreshadowing of the genocides perpetrated in the 20th century. In 1915, defeated in South Africa, the Germans left southern Africa, leaving behind their possessions and their uniforms. Out of defiance, Herero men began wearing these abandoned military garments, and made them part of their cultural identity.

In a similar process of cultural appropriation, Herero women traditionally wear a Victorian-inspired 'long' dress, the *ohorokweva onde*, with a matching headdress shaped like symbolic cow horns. When the German missionaries first arrived in the area, they wanted the Herero women to cover their bodies, so the missionaries' wives taught them sew and make dresses using imported fabrics. The cut of these dresses is characteristic of a bygone era and rather impractical for contemporary living. A short bodice with a rounded neckline is fitted tightly below the bust and extends into a full-length gathered skirt, while the leg-of-mutton sleeves are puffed wide at the top then fitted more closely below the elbow.

The *ohorokweva onde* is cut from a patchwork of squares or rectangles of fabric, joined together in strips. *Shweshwe*, the cotton prints characteristic of southern Africa, are combined with recycled pieces from old clothes, forming a colourful mosaic. Nowadays, these dresses are generally worn on special occasions. As well as looking good, this reappropriation of historical styles is a symbol of the defiance and resilience of the men and women of Namibia.

A Herero woman in a traditional dress and headdress, made from plain and glazed cotton and synthetics. Print fabrics are reserved for the hem of the skirt. The headdress, with two horn-like protrusions at the front, symbolizes the cattle that are a source of pride and wealth for the Herero people. Namibia, 2017.

NIGERIA

MAIDEN SPIRIT COSTUME

Ude Agbogho, meaning 'Fame of the Maidens', is an annual festival held by the Igbo people of the Nri-Awka region in northern Nigeria. The *agbogho mmuo*, or 'maiden spirit', is a full-body costume worn by male dancers at the festival, designed to represent the beauty of Igbo women.

In his book *Mascarades et carnavals* (2011), Jean-Paul Colleyn describes this striking tradition. Men dress up in costumes that represent a female body, with pointed breasts and a protruding navel. The finishing touch of this costume, now much sought after by collectors, is a finely carved wooden mask, often whitened with chalk, representing the idealized face of a fair-skinned young woman. The mask is topped by an elaborate hairstyle, made of sculpted braids. The impact of the costume's success depends on the skills of two master artisans, the maskmaker and the tailor.

The *agbogho mmuo* costume is covered in appliqué and embroidered motifs, inspired by the traditional tattoos and scarifications of young Igbo women. The fabrics used are cotton or felt, and the colours chosen are almost always black, red, yellow, orange and white, with the occasional touch of green. The composition is symmetrical, with its axis down the centre of the body. The tailor covers the surface of the black fabric with rows of circles, semi-circles, waves, rectangles and bands. These traditional Igbo motifs, known as *uli*, are arranged inside a grid of stripes and squares, made from interlacing strips of

fabric. The cut-out shapes are fixed in place by clearly visible stitches and enhanced with wool embroidery. As with the *kantha* (see p. 126), the embroidery stitches are both decorative and functional. They enhance the appearance of th costume while also reinforcing the fabric, giving it strength and thickness.

Above:
Igbo dance costume. Quilted cotton, embroidered with woollen threads, felt inserts. H. 170 cm. Nigeria, c. 1950. Bruno Mignot Gallery, La Wantzenau.

Opposite:
Detail of an Igbo dance costume. Plain cotton fabrics, plain fine woollen fabrics, woollen embroidery.

BENIN

DAHOMEY APPLIQUÉ

These bold appliqué motifs are one of the most famous examples of African patchwork. Featuring unmistakable brightly coloured figures against a black ground, appliqué banners are associated with the courts of the kingdom of Abomey where the kings of the Fon people reigned, in the south of the former Dahomey, renamed the Republic of Benin in 1975, fifteen years after it gained independence.

Often recording a series of events, rather like a comic strip, these appliqué designs were commissioned by the king with the aim of enhancing his prestige and safeguarding his reign by recording the great deeds of the kingdom. Royal attributes, allegorical motifs and feats of arms were depicted on hangings, parasols, canopies and banners.

Executions, beheadings, mutilations, hand-to-hand combat with ferocious animals: some of the scenes depicted are very violent, but the stylized shapes and flat colours create a distancing effect. The appliqué is done using imported fabrics once supplied by colonial trade, such as plain or printed cottons.

Nowadays, the artisans of the Yémadjè family carry on the tradition by making hangings for tourists. Their workshop is set up in one of the courtyards of the former palace of Abomey, but this was not always the case.

In the days when the royal enclosure was out of bounds, tailors and embroiderers lived in a specific district, close to the palace. The motifs are cut out using a template, then basted in position, and sewn with turned edges. The compositions are well balanced, the cutting highly detailed, and the motifs harmoniously spaced. Other textile items produced include cotton hats with appliqué decoration (below).

The banner opposite represents Hevioso or Xevioso, a horned warrior deity who belongs to the pantheon of the Fon people. Armed with a machete and a rifle, and carrying an axe in his mouth, he is shown slaughtering the Yoruba people, enemies of the Fon. Protective amulets adorn his neck and arms.

Opposite:
Detail of an appliqué hanging. Cotton with hand-cut appliqué in multicoloured fabrics. 170 × 94 cm. Hountondji family, Fon ethnic group. Abomey, Benin, c. 1930. Courtesy of Duncan Clarke, Adire African Textiles Gallery, London.

Right:
Men's hats. Cardboard, cotton fabric, embroidered with mercerized thread. Benin. Yves Venot Collection.

MALI

PATCHWORK TUNIC

The textile artisans of Mali are produce work that is vivid and imaginative. The only requisites for setting up a business are cutting table, a few baskets filled with multicoloured scraps, some lengths of bazin fabric, a sewing machine and a set of patterns that can be adapted for a range of clients.

Hassan Gomme, the tailor photographed opposite, has skilfully blended several styles of West African dress in his tunic. The base fabric is glossy bazin, a shiny damask cotton that is extremely popular in Mali. The shape echoes that of a boubou, the traditional full-length robe worn by Malian men, except that it is closer fitting. The rounded neckline with its embroidered motifs harks back to traditional tunics, while the colourful patchwork panel takes inspiration from the garments worn by the Baye Fall sect.

In Senegal, the Sufi-inspired Mouride Muslim brotherhood of the Baye Fall is firmly rooted in Wolof culture. The inventive and subversive clothing style associated with the members of this community has influenced many textile artists and designers in West Africa. To display their disregard for worldly wealth, its members often dress in patchwork robes. As the case of the garments worn by dervishes of Central Asia (see p. 139), this is a case of patchwork being associated with humility in some cultures, despite its eye-catching appearance.

FARA FARA NI

Some Malian textile artists specialize in a patchwork technique known as *découpé* (in local French) or *fara fara ni* (in Bamanankan or Bambara). These garments were traditionally made by older women who salvaged scraps of wax print fabric and pieced them together.

Today, this technique involves assembling pieces of bazin or wax print fabric to make dresses, tunics and boubous with embroidered necklines and shirtfronts. While some of the fabric utilized is remnants from sewing workshops or dye workshops, most of it is new lengths of bazin or wax print fabric, dyed locally or industrially, then polished.

The elegant boubou worn by Sanata Magassa (see p. 100) is a piece of patchwork that is both subtle and spectacular, combining the creativity of the dyer and the skills of the tailor. First, white bazin was tied at regular intervals and dyed in two tones in a series of stages. The indigo was deliberately allowed to bleed into the paler ground fabric to create a flame-like effect that imitates an *ikat* weave. The dyed and calendered fabric was then given to a tailor, who cut it into regular strips, perpendicular to the coloured stripes, then

Above:
Young Malian girl wearing a brightly coloured dress made from pieces of bazin, a glossy damask cotton, decorated with bands of braid. Bamako, Mali. 2015.

Opposite:
Senegalese tailor Hassan Gomme wearing one of his own creations, a tunic made from a machine-sewn patchwork of glossy bazin. Bamako, Mali, 2015.

GHANA

ASAFO FLAGS

On the coastal plain of Ghana, Fanti craftsmen make military standards, known as Asafo flags, decorated with cut-out appliqué motifs and allegorical symbols. In this region once occupied by the Portuguese, Dutch and British colonial powers, the Fanti began to make these banners for use in conflicts with rival groups, taking inspiration from the flags of the Royal Navy and European shipping companies.

stitched them back together, staggering the coloured areas in order to create a chequerboard design. Once all the strips were sewn together, the garment was then cut from the pieced cloth.

The simple shape of the boubou has the advantage of not creating any offcuts, apart from the neck hole. By planning the work in advance, nothing is wasted. According to author Patricia Gérimont, this staggered chequerboard technique probably has its origins in the traditional African method of sewing narrow strips of woven cotton together to make broad lengths of cloth.

Unlike the similar appliqué hangings made in Benin (see p. 97), which are decorated on only one side, the appliqué designs on Asafo flags are added to both sides so they can be viewed from any angle. The motifs are cut out in pairs and arranged as mirror images. An alternative, more time-consuming method involves inlaying the cut-out motif in a hole cut through the base fabric. Motifs range from lettered inscriptions, regimental numbers, military scenes, rebus puzzles and symbols. Simple but striking, the motifs stand out boldly against red, yellow, green, black or pink grounds, depending on the regiment. The fabrics used are generally imported.

Over time, the Union Jack flag, often depicted in patchwork in one of the corners, was gradually replaced by the red, yellow and green flag of Ghana; this change allows Asafo flags to be accurately dated. Some flags include a patchwork border, usually in red and black or black and white checks, edged with a row of fringing.

Left:
Sanata Magassa wears a boubou and headwrap made from a patchwork created by cutting strips of bazin fabric dyed with stripes and rearranging them in a staggered pattern.

Opposite, top:
Asafo flag made by Baba Issah (1916–1991) at the Swedru workshop. Cotton fabric, depicting an armed spirit of the bush with six heads, framed by rows of red and white squares, with a Union Jack in the corner. 95 × 150 cm. Ghana, 1950s. Courtesy of Duncan Clarke, Adire African Textiles Gallery, London.

Opposite, below:
A selection of Asafo flags, created in different workshops. Cotton fabrics, c. 100 × 160 cm. Ghana, 1950s. Courtesy of Duncan Clarke, Adire African Textiles Gallery, London.

Nº6 COMP.

Nº 2 Cº

Nº 6 COMPANY ANAMABOE

Nº I

Nº 6 Cº ANOMABU

Nº I Cº AXIM

DEMOCRATIC REPUBLIC OF THE CONGO

N'TCHAK

Unlike West Africa, Central Africa had no cotton, silk or wool for many years, other than in the form of imports. Clothing fabrics were traditionally made of beaten bark, raffia fibre and animal skins. These textiles were also worn for festivals, dances and funeral rituals, and were even traded as currency.

The Kuba community live in the Kasai region, in what was formerly known as Zaire but which is now the Democratic Republic of the Congo, on the edge of the equatorial forest. They make traditional skirts (*n'tchak*) using a cloth made from raffia palm fibres. The fibres are exposed and then dried, then cut into thin strips. Men weave the fibre, using it for both warp and weft. The short lengths of the fibre mean that the panels are small, so they must be sewn edge to edge to create larger pieces. Women dye the raffia using natural plant dyes, then sew the pieces together and finally apply the decoration. A common way to sew the panels together is a chequerboard of alternating colours. It is interesting to note that the raffia panels are stitched together on the right side,

Below, top:
Dance skirt (*n'tchak*).
Unbleached raffia. Folded
seams sewn on the right side.
Appliqué motifs in dyed raffia,
edged with embroidery
stitches. Edges bound with
a strip of raffia. 65 × 220 cm.

Kuba, Ngeendé or Ngongo
ethnic group. Democratic
Republic of the Congo.
Nicole Roca Collection.

Below, centre:
Dance skirt (*n'tchak*). Dyed
raffia with appliqué motifs in

unbleached raffia. 55 × 175 cm.
Kuba, Ngeendé or Ndongo
ethnic group. Democratic
Republic of the Congo.
Nicole Roca Collection.

Below, bottom and overleaf:
Dance skirt (*n'tchak*). Woven

raffia. 8 blocks of chequerboard
patchwork, 8 with eyelet
stitch embroidery, openwork,
seeds and cowrie shells. Braid
and tasselled edge. 50 ×
200 cm. Democratic Republic
of the Congo. Tuulikki
Chompré Collection.

using folded seams. This added texture forms a key part of the decoration, in a way similar to the Korean *bojagi* (see p. 150).

Using appliqué techniques, Kuba women decorate the fabric with abstract shapes cut from raffia cloth, and dyed a contrasting colour. Smaller round pieces are sometimes scattered across the fabric to hide holes. The rows of stitching around the edges of each shape are an integral part of the aesthetics of the cloth. Behind the apparently random placing of the asymmetric motifs lies a hidden balance, the shapes slotting together to create carefully arranged negative spaces. A long *n'tchak* unfurls like a parchment scroll, covered in intriguing symbols. Similar motifs are used to adorn wooden sculptures, wall paintings and in body scarifications.

As well as the appliqué motifs favoured by the Kuba people, these raffia cloths may also be decorated in other styles, including the renowned 'Kasai velvet' embroidery practised by the Shoowa people. From the 1930s onwards, production of these traditional textiles in these regions was often overseen by missionaries. There are many examples of these fabrics in circulation today, both authentic and copies.

Below and opposite (detail): Barkcloth skirt (*tapa*). Patchwork with folded seams on the reverse. 45 × 200 cm. Democratic Republic of the Congo. Tuulikki Chompré Collection.

TAPA

While Kuba garments of raffia are relatively common, those made of barkcloth are more rare. The prestigious textile shown opposite and below was designed to be draped around the body during the funeral. Known as a *tapa*, it is made up of a mosaic of small triangles, cut from the peeled bark of a tropical fig tree.

The inner layer of the bark is dampened and pounded with a textured wooden beater to flatten it. Then the ochre-coloured beaten bark, which is now much softer, is dyed white and black. Despite the simple tools used to make it, the finished cloth is a real feat of precision.

Rather like a Western patchwork quilt, the cloth shown here is made up of individually made blocks. Fifteen dark blocks alternate with fifteen paler blocks, each block being made from fifteen squares, and each square incorporating four right-angled triangles. The centre of each block is marked by a motif in the alternate colourway. The combination of plant dyes and the natural colour of the raffia creates a bold graphic look that recalls the Op art movement and artists such as Victor Vasarely. As a final touch, the geometric composition is edged with a double border.

CAMEROON

BAMUM TUNICS

'They wear boubous of different lengths one on top of the other, they're all coloured prints and different embroideries, they eventually bring together a surprising ensemble in very good taste with the orange, the blue, the gold or the white predominant.' – Blaise Cendrars, *Les Boubous* (1924)

The Bamum (or Bamoun) people originate from the Grasslands region in western Cameroon. Large public gatherings, such as the annual Lela festival in Bali Nyonga, provide an opportunity to observe a huge variety of traditional garments being worn by men and women.

It is likely that earlier Bamum garments, like many West African textiles, were composed of narrow strips of woven fabric, sewn selvedge to selvedge. It is possible to trace the development of Bamum clothing through garments conserved in museums and postcards dating from the colonial era. With its characteristic T-shape, the traditional loose tunic is now cut from industrially produced cotton, usually dyed black, rather than the earlier handwoven indigo. Similarly, complex embroidered motifs have been superseded by appliqué cut-outs. On the other hand, some features remain the same, including the rows of embroidered 'chicken feet' motifs that often surround the neckline.

The round neckline is often set inside a square frame, with its points facing downwards. Sleeves, which may be long or short, are highlighted with rows of motifs that are repeated around the bottom edge of the garment. Several details differentiate these Grasslands tunics from the more voluminous

babban riga tunics worn by the Hausa people, including the lack of breast pockets, the symmetrical placement of motifs, and identical back and front designs.

The appliqué motifs are cut from white, red or yellow mass-produced cotton. The source of these designs is not always obvious. In the book dedicated to the textile collection of Zaira and Marcel Mis, *Costumes et textiles d'Afrique* (2008), the authors discuss the motif of a highly stylized spider, a popular symbol among the people of the Grasslands; associated with wisdom, it is used in traditional divination rituals and has been found carved on royal stools. Other patterns are comparable to the resist-dyed motifs found on *ndop* textiles (see p. 111).

The appliqué fabric is positioned on top of the base fabric, tacked in place, then the designs are cut out. The edges are turned and hemmed by hand or machine. For ease of working, the motifs are added to the flat fabric pieces before the side seams and sleeves of the garment are sewn up. Curved and circular shapes, which may represent the eyes of a spider, are particularly time-consuming to render in this technique, and as can be seen on the designs illustrated here, the results are often slightly uneven. A similar chevron pattern to the one featured on the long tunic can be seen on a Banjara blouse from India (see p. 130): a neat coincidence, thousands of kilometres apart.

Opposite, above:
Woman's tunic. Mass-produced cotton with machine-sewn appliqué. H. 110 cm, width 140 cm. Cameroon. Liliane and Armel Chichery Collection.

Opposite, below:
Dignitary's tunic. Mass-produced cotton with machine-sewn appliqué. H. 110 cm, width 200 cm. Cameroon. Liliane and Armel Chichery Collection.

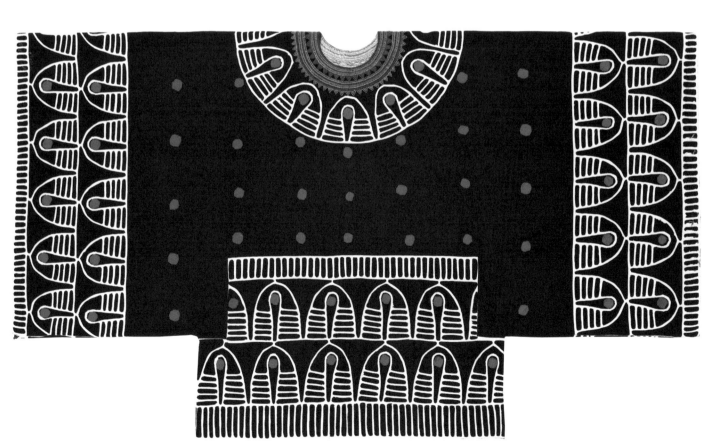

NDOP TUNIC

This is not a skirt but a tunic worn by men. When Bamileke dancers take part in a ceremonial performance, the fabric whirls out, opening like a flower and revealing the red vents beneath the indigo pleats. However, this garment began its life as a simple rectangle of fabric.

Ndop cloth is a traditional fabric from the Grasslands region of Cameroon. Once restricted to the elite, it is now worn at festivals, funerals and celebrations of any kind. It also forms part of daily life, as shown by the creations of many contemporary artisans and designers who have been inspired by its blue and white designs.

This fabric is the product of a complex network of skills that connects several different communities throughout Cameroon. Cotton cultivation and spinning are practised in the north of the country, while weaving is carried out by craftsmen living on the Nigerian border, on the banks of the Bénoué River. Narrow strips known as *leppi* or *gabaga* are woven by men using treadle looms. Once the strips are sewn, the cloth is transported to the homeland of the Bamileke people. Here, artisans use charcoal to draw motifs on the fabric. These are then overstitched using raffia thread, so that those areas will be protected during resist-dyeing. The bundles of unbleached cloth are then sent back to Garoua, in the north, and handed over to the specialist indigo dyers. The dyed cloth is then returned to the Grasslands, where the resist stitching is removed, revealing the white patterns on the indigo ground. The *ndop* is finally ready to be sold.

The incorporation of red fabric is still a subject of speculation. Depending on the garment, it may take the form of felted wool or imported cotton. In either case, its texture contrasts with the hand-woven *ndop* fabric, while the red shade stands out boldly against the deep indigo. In this tunic, triangular pieces of red cotton and felt from various sources have been inserted to form vents. The same shade of madder red is often used on the borders of tunics, dance skirts and large hangings. Here, the colour may symbolize blood. As for its origin, an interesting hypothesis has been put forward: it may be a reappropriation of the long red belts of felted wool that were worn by Senegalese riflemen during the First World War. Several photographs archived at the Fondation Albert Kahn in Paris show these belts being worn as part of the uniforms of African recruits.

Above and opposite (detail): Ndop tunic. Locally produced cotton, woven in narrow strips, and resist-stitched before indigo dyeing. Red cotton and wool. 78 × 72 cm, full width 300 cm. Cameroon. Liliane and Armel Chichery Collection.

SUDAN

MAHDI ARMY *JIBBEH*

**In the late 19th century, Sudan was
under the rule of Egypt, which itself was
dependent on the Ottoman Empire. In
1881, Sudanese leader Mohammed Ibn
el-Sayyid Abdullah (1844–1885) proclaimed
himself Mahdi, a descendant of the Prophet
Muhammad. He was highly critical of
other Muslim leaders, whom he accused
of corruption, as well as of the Egyptian
regime that governed Sudan, and his
followers formed an army of liberation.
In 1882, the conflict forced the British,
anxious to protect their interests on
the Suez Canal, to intervene.**

In order to standardize the different factions
fighting the Egyptians and the British, the
uniform chosen for the officers of the Mahdi
Army was an unbleached cotton *jibbeh*.
Inspired by the patched robes worn by some
Sufi dervishes, this uniform was decorated
with appliqué rectangles, a motif symbolizing
humility. According to research undertaken by
the Smithsonian Museum in Washington DC,
the patches were probably made from fabric
recycled from enemy uniforms, conferring on
the tunic a protective and commemorative
function, in the wake of a series of victories
over the Anglo-Egyptian forces. This success
did not last long, however, as Mahdi died
in 1885. His successor, Khalifa al-Mahdi,
transformed the Mahdist movement into a
state, but died in 1899, after failing to prevent
the reconquest of Sudan by Britain.

Now conserved in private collections,
the *jibbeh* of the Mahdi Army are all identical
in shape: a T-shaped tunic, broader at the
bottom, made of three strips: a central
rectangle with two trapezoids at the sides.

The sleeves are set in. The decorative appliqué
takes the form of several large rectangles on
the front and back panels, and around each
sleeve. Each oblong is edged with braid in
a contrasting shade. The rectangles on the
side panels are surmounted by dark-coloured
arrow-like motifs, outlined with braid. A round
neckhole allows the tunic to be pulled over the
head. The neckline is edged with braid and
strengthened with an extra layer of appliqué,
cut to form a tapering point. The cuffs and
hem are edged with piping and braid,
a practical but elegant touch.

Tunic (*jibbeh*). Unbleached cotton fabric spun and woven locally, with appliqué motifs in green, red and dark blue cotton. Small pockets with piped edges. Arrowhead appliqué motifs have been added to the side panels. H. 100 cm, width 133 cm. Sudan, late 19th century. Galerie Patrick & Ondine Mestdagh, Brussels.

MAURITANIA

TUAREG SANDALS & BAGS

The Tuareg people traditionally live a nomadic existence across a vast area of the Sahara desert. When crossing the desert, leather sandals (*naïls*) provide vital protection from the burning ground. Flat and lightweight, they can easily be slipped off at the entrance to a tent or a mosque. Their broad soles protect against the bites of scorpions or snakes, as well as spiny desert plants.

Herds of goats, sheep, cows and camels make it possible for the Tuareg to manufacture a wide range of leather items, including sandals, waterskins, saddles, cushions and bags of all kinds. Many of these are simple in shape but elaborate in their decoration. Production begins by tanning the skins to create supple and lightweight leather. This is followed by dyeing, cutting and glueing, tasks generally performed by female leatherworkers.

Sandal soles and the flaps of bags are often covered with inlaid geometric patterns cut from different shades of leather. Equipped with a blade, a smoother and a polisher, a compass, an awl, and a leather fingerguard for protection, the leatherworker cuts, inlays and glues, using fine leather laces to stitch the pieces in place as an embroiderer would. A goat's hair brush and dishes made from large shells complete the traditional array of tools.

The straps of the sandals shown above are finely decorated and held by a button, trimmed with a tassel. The bags are fastened with a loop and button. The straps are often braided, with leather fringes hanging from the bags and swaying as the wearer walks.

Small leather pouches are often worn around the neck, and densely adorned with inlaid, embroidered and fringed decoration. Emerald green is a particularly popular colour for dyed leather. Every motif has a meaning, elevating all these accessories beyond their utilitarian function. As for the sandals, the decoration concealed beneath the sole of the foot is believed to the wearer from any dangers they may encounter en route.

This inlaid leatherwork is only tangentially related to patchwork, but it is similarly functional and decorative, requiring nimble fingers, careful planning and a great deal of imagination.

Above:
Tuareg sandals. Dyed lambskin with cow or zebu leather sole. L. 29 cm. Mauritania. Liliane and Armel Chichery Collection.

Opposite:
Detail of interlacing and sewing on a Tuareg bag. Leather and strips of dyed skins. Mauritania. Liliane and Armel Chichery Collection.

EGYPT

APPLIQUÉ HANGINGS

These decorative fabric hangings were made in the Bab al-Zuwayla district of Cairo, on Shari' Khayamiyya (or Suq Al-Khayamiyya) Street. Artisans and their apprentices, usually male, cut and sewed these pieces by hand, alongside a wide range of cushion covers, banners, door curtains and bedspreads intended for both the domestic and tourist markets.

The discovery of similar hangings in the tomb of Tutankhamun in the 1920s suggests that this craft dates back to at least 1300 BCE. This tradition is associated with that of the *qanat*, a type of canopy or panel curtain, often decorated with appliqué patterns and hung on the outer walls of Egyptian houses for special occasions. These hangings were used to welcome friends and neighbours to celebrate a wedding, a circumcision, a religious festival. Popular motifs included Islamic arabesques and interlacing, and even lines from the Qur'an.

The tourist boom that followed the discovery of Tutankhamun's tomb led the craftsmen of Cairo to expand their range and to include motifs inspired by the mythology of ancient Egypt. Sold in Cairo, Luxor and Port Said, these textiles made ideal souvenirs.

The panels illustrated here, which date from the 1950s, are skilfully crafted. Sewn on an unbleached cotton support, sometimes handwoven, the delicate colours of the appliqué motifs are derived from vegetable dyes including indigo or madder. Cut out with the aid of templates, the motifs have turned edges and are enhanced with embroidered details. Despite the formulaic nature of the overall designs, these creations are carefully executed with great skill.

Despite a recent decline in tourist numbers, this delicate craft still survives and men can still be found sewing near Bab al-Zuwayla, one of Cairo's gates, built in 1092. Sadly, however, the traditional appliqué hangings are now being replaced with cheaper printed versions.

Opposite:
Detail of a wall hanging. Locally woven unbleached cotton with appliqué motifs in indigo, madder, brown and black dyed cotton. Additional embroidery. 91 × 45 cm. Egypt, c. 1950. Catherine Legrand Collection.

Below:
Wall hanging with a mythological scene. Handmade unbleached and dyed cotton. Appliqué motifs with additional embroidery. 175 × 47 cm. Egypt, c. 1950. Liliane and Armel Chichery Collection.

IRAN

QAMIS & SHALVAR

Was this boldly coloured ensemble created as a result of political discrimation? The answer may well be yes. According to several sources, including Fahmida Suleman's *Textiles of the Middle East and Central Asia* (2017) and Jennifer Wearden and Patricia L. Baker's *Iranian Textiles* (2010), an Iranian law of the 19th century prohibited Zoroastrians from buying fabric by the yard. As a result, the women of this community started circumventing the ban by making magnificent patchwork garments from small pieces of fabric.

It is to these creative and clever women that we owe this colourful tunic (*qamis*) and matching loose trousers (*shalvar*), made from vertical bands of fabric. The outfit would have been completed with a cap (*lachak*) and a head veil (*bach*), both embroidered. Everyday garments were generally made without the added embroidery.

The costume shown opposite was designed for a special occasion, probably a wedding. The dominant colours are green and red, which were believed to be auspicious. The tunic and trousers are made from a patchwork of silks and cottons that have been embroidered to create the illusion of a printed fabric. This technique is known as 'Zoroastrian embroidery' (*zartoshti duzi*). The trousers feature no fewer than seven different shades of silk, embroidered with sun motifs (a male symbol) alternating with cats with their tails in the air (a female symbol). The coloured bands of the tunic are embroidered with tiny dots, forming a horizontal zigzag pattern.

The patchwork band shown on the right consists of narrow pieces of printed fabric,

4 to 6 cm wide, separated by piped braid. It was traditional for young women to prepare their own wedding trousseau in advance, which would include multicoloured patchwork blocks that could be sewn together to create a wedding costume.

A monotheistic faith, Zoroastrianism developed in Iran in the 7th century BCE, then became the official religion of the Sassanian Empire before the advent of Islam. Many Zoroastrians subsequently converted to Islam, while others sought refuge in India. There are now around 40,000 Zoroastrians in Iran, mainly in Tehran, Yazd and Kerman.

Right:
Detail of a patchwork band, made from cotton prints alternated with embroidered silk. 145 × 45 cm. Iran, c. 1900. Dominique Niorthe Collection.

Opposite:
Woman's tunic and baggy trousers. Embroidered silk and cotton. Tunic: H. 100, w. 97 cm; trousers: H. 92 cm, leg width 63 cm. Iran, 1850–1900. British Museum, London.

SYRIA

Below, from top to bottom:
Cushion. Striped and printed
cotton fabrics. 84 × 40 cm.
Syria, c. 1950. Catherine
Legrand Collection.

Woman's coat (*dura'a*). Coarse
cotton with silk appliqué and
embroidery. H. 138 cm, width
125 cm. Syria, c. 1950. Liliane
and Armel Chichery Collection.

Opposite:
Detail of the inner lining of
a woman's coat (*dura'a*).
Indigo-dyed cotton with
reverse appliqué in black
ottoman and cotton. White
thread. Idlib region, Syria.
Liliane and Armel Chichery
Collection.

DURA'A & CUSHION

**It has been suggested that the appliqué
designs sometimes concealed in the lining
of traditional Syrian coats may once have
had some form of sexual connotation. While
this explanation remains unconfirmed, the
motifs are indisputably striking.**

The woman's coat on the right, the *dura'a*, is a
style reserved for special occasions. Cut from
a heavy indigo cotton, its plastron and sleeves
are embroidered with cross-stitch motifs in
pearlized or mercerized cotton. However, it is
the lining that draws the eye. The back of the
lower pocket is made from a square of black
cotton with reverse appliqué cut-outs that
reveal a red silk *ikat* weave beneath. The front
edges and hem of the coat, meanwhile, are
lined with appliqué pieces of silk satin woven
in Aleppo or Damascus, with yellow and red
warp *ikat* motifs. Elsewhere, this type of lining
might have been added to strengthen the
garment, but in this particular case, the lining
fabrics are more valuable and delicate than
the coarse outer fabric. We might therefore
speculate that it is a hidden form of decoration,
revealed only to those close to the wearer.

The lining of the *dura'a* shown opposite is
another mystery. The decoration is only visible
when the sides are opened, to reveal a maze-
like motif in reverse appliqué, made by cutting,
hollowing and hemming an indigo fabric.
Although the turned edges of the cut-outs are
stitched in black, which is invisible on the black
silk ottoman, the work is studded with white
topstitching that evokes stars on a dark night.

According to Marie-Bénédicte Seynhaeve,
former curator of the textile collections at the
Musée Bargoin in Clermont-Ferrand, France,
this decoration was made by the farming

women of Kafr Takharim and is specific to the
region of Idlib. The indigo fabrics, meanwhile,
apparently come from Aleppo where there was
an active association of indigo dyers before
the First World War.

The rectangular Syrian cushion shown
above is made from a selection of cottons
and satins, with a backing of red fabric. The
stepped cut-out motifs are outlined with
a narrow cotton braid in a contrasting
colour, couched into place.

PALESTINE

JILLAYEH

The *jillayeh* is a long coat-dress worn by women, often embroidered, with a front opening and elbow-length sleeves. It is worn with trousers over a white belted tunic. While the *jillayeh* is best known for the intricacy of its embroidery, those from the region of Galilee, near Nazareth, are notable for combining embroidery with appliqué motifs.

Both the front and the back of this coat-dress in coarse indigo-dyed fabric are decorated with appliqué squares in green, red and yellow cotton. With their randomly cut-out lines, the squares resemble falling leaves, or perhaps the paper cut-out collages created by Henri Matisse. The same appliqué technique is also found on cushion covers. The pieces may be cut from cotton, silk taffeta (*heremzi*) or leftover pieces of silk *ikat* woven in neighbouring Syria. The motifs are carefully sewn with coloured threads and heavy stitches that are clearly visible on the reverse, suggesting that the coat-dress was intended to be reversible.

This style of dress, reserved for special occasions, was traditionally made to measure by a seamstress who assembled pieces that had been embroidered or appliquéd beforehand, hence its name *jillayeh tafsilé* ('made to order'). In 1991, an archaeological dig in Asi-al-Hadath, a cave in the Lebanese mountains, led to the discovery of around thirty dresses dating from the end of the 13th century. They were made from cotton fabric dyed with indigo and walnut dye, and some featured plastrons decorated with geometric embroidery in red and black silk. These finds are an excellent demonstration of the longevity of this style of garment, which has withstood the test of time for hundreds of years.

Throughout these centuries, the women of rural Palestine have continued to work the land, watch their herds and keep their textile traditions alive, embroidering wedding dresses, veils, linen, handkerchiefs, tobacco pouches and cushions. Today, for many women, embroidery remains an act of resistance, a means of asserting a cultural identity via the needle. Local craft associations offer mutual support and allow women to use their creations to achieve a level of financial independence.

Right and opposite (detail): Coat-dress (*jillayeh*). Indigo cotton base. Front opening, cuffs and hem adorned with a band of green and yellow patchwork squares, sewn point to point. Appliqué motif of cut-out squares in green, yellow and red silk taffeta. H. 141 cm, w. 84 cm. Galilee, 19th century. British Museum, London.

ASIA

Perhaps it is the vast, wild landscapes, ranging from towering peaks to the driest of deserts, that have inspired such a rich variety of textiles across Central Asia and the Indian subcontinent. Decorating homes, making wedding trousseaus and children's clothes – these responsibilities traditionally fell to women, who often spent long hours on needlework. Although they had limited means, their sense of invention knew no bounds. This chapter explores the region's rich history of textile art and its survival into a present shaped by globalization and mass production.

The process of making the traditional costumes of Korea requires great expertise and is governed by a strict set of rules. From the *hanbok* to the *bojagi*, many types of Korean textiles feature a subtle use of patchwork. In Japan, we will explore the world of *boro*, textiles that are mended or patched together. The north of Japan is home to more treasures, such as the decorative appliqué motifs that the Ainu people embroider onto their clothes.

Among the minority peoples who live in the mountain areas of China, Vietnam and Laos, traditional patchwork and appliqué techniques continue to flourish. They remain a part of daily life for many women who proudly preserve their own cultural identities by making and wearing garments that represent their ethnic group, their village or their social status.

INDIA

KANTHA

The traditional craft of *kantha* is about making something new from something old. For many years, this folk art was little known outside of India, at least beyond a few collectors. It involves recycling old saris and *dhotis* (traditional men's clothing) to make quilts. Reusing clothing in this way was also commonplace among American pioneers, although with one key difference – the rectangular lengths of sari fabric are even better suited to the purpose.

Not all *kantha* is the same. The most impressive examples come from Kolkata and are made by recycling pieces of *khadi* – unbleached cotton that is spun and woven locally. The women allow their imaginations and their needles to run riot across these expanses of cotton, using running stitch to depict scenes of daily life or religious imagery inspired by the *Mahabharata* or the *Ramayana*. Pratima Devi, daughter-in-law of the Bengali poet Rabindranath Tagore, was impressed by these works and was responsible for a *kantha* revival in the 1940s.

Although *kantha* is practised across India, it remains a humble art. The cloths are used as quilts or for humble household tasks, such as cleaning or wrapping items. Although it has existed for centuries, the importance of *kantha* as a craft has also only recently begun to be appreciated, in a similar way to the *boro* revival in Japan (see pp. 152–157). *Kantha* is now inspiring designers both in India and abroad, and the practice is supported by humanitarian organizations working with Indian women.

The first step in the process is to wash the fabrics, then they are sorted into three categories: the finest are used on the outside, the less well-preserved for filling, and the largest pieces are reserved for the backing. The pieces are then handstitched together, with the seamstress drawing on her own taste and experience to decide which scraps of fabric to place alongside each other: combining different prints, using complementary or contrasting colours, playing with different shapes, and concealing any tears or worn areas. Instead of using a quilting frame, the three layers are arranged on a mat on the ground for quilting. The seamstress does not use a ruler or measuring tape or follow a pattern. Instead, she measures everything by eye, using the distance from elbow to fingertips, the span from thumb to little finger, or the width of a finger, to determine how much space to leave between topstitches. She then quilts the three layers together using a long continuous length of thread, most commonly off-white, although sometimes another colour is chosen to match or constrast with the fabric. She begins by quilting a line running parallel to the longest side of the piece and – unlike in Western quilting – starts at the edge and works her way towards the centre. As an enduring folk art, *kantha* now allows many women to maintain a degree of financial independence.

Above:
Kantha dowry bag. Cotton decorated with topstitch. 62 × 55 cm. India. Liliane and Armel Chichery Collection.

Opposite, above:
Detail of *kantha* quilt. Used synthetics and cotton. 136 × 176 cm. India. Amit Zadok Collection.

Opposite, below:
Detail of *kantha* quilt. Cotton. 172 × 240 cm. India. Catherine Legrand Collection.

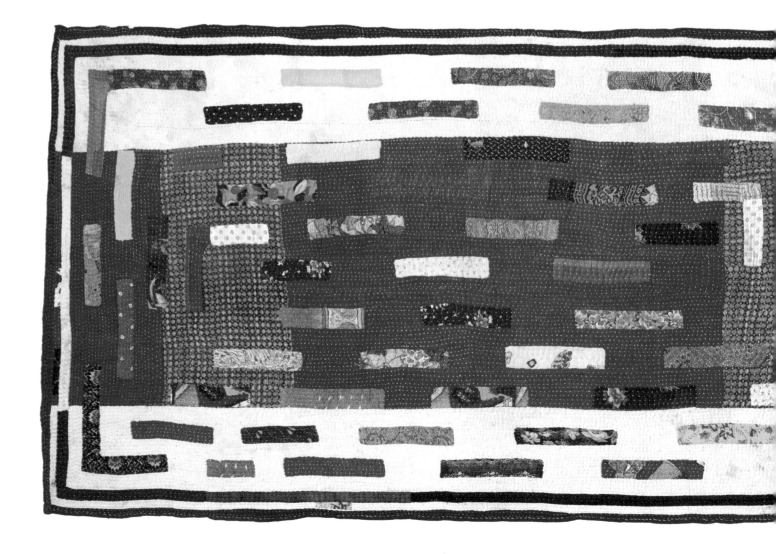

GODRI

Godri quilts, which originate from Gujarat, have many functions. When spread over a *charpoy* – a bed made of interwoven strips hung between a frame – they become mattresses. They can also be used as bedcovers or bedside rugs, rolled up and used as pillows or bolsters, or hung on a wall to provide privacy. Even when they are worn out, they can be reused as cushioning under a camel's packsaddle.

Among rural populations, *godri* quilts often form part of a bride's dowry. Brides sew them before the wedding to bring to their new home, and are given more as gifts. They also take great care over sewing *godri* for their children. The *godri* are folded and stacked on a clothes chest, covered with a special cloth – the *dharaniyo* – to protect them from dust. A similar tradition exists in Slovakia, the Czech Republic, Hungary, Poland and Russia, where brides display their handiwork – sheets, tablecloths, cushions – on top of their marriage chests for everyone to admire.

The colourful baby blanket (below left) was made by a woman from the Gadhavi community in Saurashtra, Gujarat. She sewed borders of white fabric on either side of the wide central band, then added appliqué patches of cloth, probably taken from old saris. The design displays a keen sense of space, rhythm and colour. The spontaneous feel and simplicity of this work, which doesn't feature any additional embroidery or mirrors, as well as the use of recycled fabrics, is reminiscent of the quilts made by African American communities in the southern US (see p. 74).

The white *godri* decorated with dancing figures (opposite above) was made by a woman from the Bhopa community, who live in the Dwarka region of Gujarat. Arrranged around the central floral motif, there are two stylized female figures, each carrying a jar on her head, two temple motifs and two swastikas, an ancient symbol of wellbeing. Stylized flowers fill the rest of the space. All the coloured motifs have been appliqué stitched onto the white ground. The blanket has also been hand-quilted with concentric rectangles in running stitch.

Opposite, above:
Bedcover (*godri*). Cotton and synthetic fabrics. 111 × 188 cm. Bhopa community. Dwarka, Gujarat, India. Catherine Legrand Collection.

Opposite, below:
Baby blanket (*godri*). Cotton. 79 × 115 cm. Gadhvi community. Saurashtra, Gujarat, India, c. 1950. Catherine Legrand Collection.

Above:
Umra Kahana, a woman from the village of Hodka, selling *ralli* and *godri*. Kutch, Gujarat, India.

PHETIYA & KANCHALI

The Banjara are a semi-nomadic people who are spread out across many states in India. Once upon a time, they travelled around the Indian subcontinent in their caravans, supplying the Mughal army with salt and grain, and they have retained a reputation as merchants.

Fiercely proud of their heritage, Banjara women offer irrefutable proof that clothing is a reflection of identity. Their embroidered skirts, sequinned veils, jewelry and tattoos are highly distinctive.

Banjara women traditionally wear *phetiyas* – long, full, pleated skirts, most of which are sumptuously embroidered and decorated with mirrors. The *phetiya* shown here is unusual, as it is decorated exclusively with appliqué motifs rather than traditional embroidery. The band of fabric around the hem of the skirt – called a *lawan* – is 4 metres long. It features a white herringbone pattern on a black ground, between two rows of triangular motifs. V-shapes have been cut into the white cotton to reveal the black ground beneath, and the cut edges are turned. The tips are crowned with small embroidered motifs, making them look like temples. The same white pyramid-like pattern is repeated on the next row up, where it is dominated by taller spire-like shapes, also created using reverse appliqué. Finally, white cut-out appliqué motifs are scattered across the skirt in an apparently random fashion. Each of these is made from a single square of cotton, folded and cut through to form a radial design. Once these motifs are unfolded and their edges turned, they resemble flowers, stars, spider's webs or snowflakes. As Charlotte Kwon, co-author of *Textiles of the Banjara* (2016), points out, these reverse appliqué techniques are similar to those found on *godris* and *rallis* in Sindh, Rajasthan and Gujarat (see pp. 128 and 134).

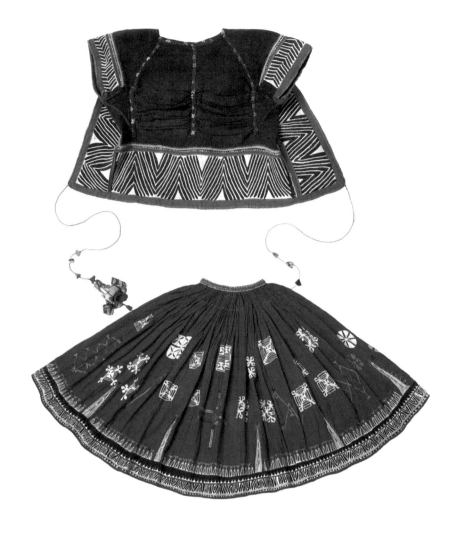

The fitted bodice shown above is called a *kanchali*. The black cotton fabric is pleated to fit around the bust, and long braids adorned with small tassels allow it to be tied in place while leaving the wearer's back elegantly bare. It is decorated with a herringbone motif around the waist and back opening, and around both sleeves. These patterns are created using reverse appliqué, like the motifs on the *phetiya*.

Above:
Bodice (*kanchali*). Cotton. Banjara community. India. Liliane and Armel Chichery Collection.

Below and opposite (detail):
Skirt (*phetiya*). Cotton. H. 85 cm, total width 400 cm. Banjara community. Khandesh, India. Liliane and Armel Chichery Collection.

THIGMA GONCHA
& THIGMA PABU

This stunning coat-dress, the rear of which is shown here, is called a *thigma goncha*. These unusual garments are worn only by the nomadic women who live in the high-altitude valleys of Rupshu in eastern Ladakh. Made from hand-spun wool serge, the garment protects its wearer against the harsh climate. It is made from narrow panels stitched side by side, with additional panels sewn into the waist to make the skirt flare out.

Above and opposite (detail):
Coat-dress (*thigma goncha*).
Wool serge. Made of 30
narrow panels dyed in different
colours. H. 135 cm, w. 147 cm,
full width 560 cm. Rupshupa
community, Ladakh.
Catherine Legrand Collection.

Right:
Boots (*thigma pabu*).
Wool uppers, leather soles.
Rupshupa community, Ladakh.
Catherine Legrand Collection.

Plant-based dyes – indigo, mulberry, madder and rhubarb – are used to create the subtle and varied colour palette, with some shades obtained by dyeing the cloth twice. The panels are arranged in alternating colours – green, indigo, aubergine, purple, violet and burgundy – with creative colour combinations also used on the sleeves.

The round motifs – four cross-like petals within a circle of a different colour – are created using a tie-dye technique, known locally as *thigma*. The fabric panels are dyed before being stitched together. The same technique is used on shawls, woollen shoes, belts and saddle covers. According to ethnographer Catherine Mangeot, these decorative techniques – which are found throughout the Himalayas – can be traced back to the spread of Vajrayana Buddhism from its spiritual centre in Lhasa.

The boots below, called *thigma pabu*, are made from wool, with a thick leather sole. They are lined with undyed wool, and decorated on the outside, like the dress, with cross motifs inside circles of a different shade. The curved toes are a feature often found in cold climates; they help to protect the wearer's toes from getting damp in the rain or snow.

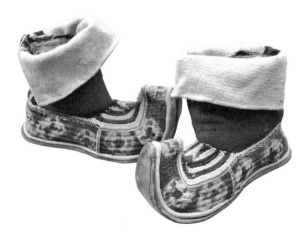

INDIA & PAKISTAN

RALLI

These quilts, decorated with lace-like appliqué motifs, are sewn by women from the Mahar community of Sindh and southern Punjab. In neighbouring Gujarat, women of the Meghwal community and the Muslim Banni people who live in the desert region called the Rann of Kutch are prolific patchworkers and quilters. When sewing a wedding trousseau, women often hold a gathering called a *ralli-vijhanu*, especially when it is time to lay out the full piece and quilt the layers together.

The name of the quilt often comes from the number of squares or blocks (called *guls*, meaning 'flowers') that it consists of. Patchwork and reverse appliqué are often used on the same quilt. The artisans of the Meghwal and Mahar communities make *ralli* from squares or triangles of fabric stitched together to form larger blocks, alternating with squares decorated with cut-out motifs, created using a reverse appliqué technique known as *kutab* (from the English 'cut up'). In the quilt shown opposite, the border is made up of single-colour bands, separated by a patchwork row of triangles and squares turned diagonally so they stand on one corner. Older pieces of fabric are used as filling for the quilt. If there is a large enough piece of fabric to hand, it will be used for the backing; if not, multiple pieces will be joined together using running stitch.

Above:
Small wall hanging. Cotton. 80 × 80 cm. Gujarat, India. Tuulikki Chompré Collection.

Opposite:
Detail of a *ralli* quilt. Cotton coloured with plant-based dyes. Patchwork and appliqué. 220 × 110 cm. Sindh, Pakistan. Tuulikki Chompré Collection.

TUKRI

Despite their historical, political and religious differences, India and Pakistan share a rich textile heritage that includes woodblock-print fabrics, embroidery and patchwork quilts.

In his book *Indian Textiles* (2014), John Gillow records how quilting techniques were introduced to Pakistan by British and American missionaries in the second half of the 19th century. Many Muslim and Hindu women embraced these crafts and made them their own, becoming highly skilful and creative quilters. Padded quilts and large bags soon became regular additions to wedding dowries.

Tukri is a formal style of patchwork quilt, featuring coloured squares arranged in diagonal lines in order to create diamond shapes that radiate from one or more central points. The fabric is usually cotton in block colours – red, yellow, black and white. The colours are sometimes faded with exposure to sunlight. Historically, the fabrics were once dyed using indigo, turmeric and madder root, but now synthetic dyes are used. The squares of fabric, called *chand*, are cut out and stitched into blocks by hand. The central field is traditionally edged with a toothed border motif called *kungri*.

Above and opposite (detail): Tukri quilt. Cotton. 168 × 121 cm. Maldhari community. Kutch, Gujarat, India. Wahid Wazir Collection.

BACHAKADIYO & KHOTALO

These beautifully embellished bags were once a vital part of nomadic life, and they are still used today in the wedding ceremonies of several different ethnic groups. They are traditionally sewn and embroidered by the bride, her mother and her sisters. The larger bags, called _khotalo_, are used to store clothing and gifts, while the smaller, envelope-shaped purses, called _bachakadiyo_, contain the bride's jewelry. After the wedding, these bags are put to daily use in the home.

Different communities have developed their own decorative styles, embellishing the bags with patchwork motifs, appliqué, embroidery, mirrors, shells, buttons and tassels. The bags shown here were all sewn using similar techniques to those used for bedcovers (see p. 136). They are made up of squares arranged in a chequerboard pattern, with motifs created using appliqué or reverse appliqué, and are lined, quilted, piped and sometimes embroidered.

This style of envelope-shaped purse, known as a _bachakadiyo_ in the Rann of Kutch in India, is found in many cultures, including Uzbekistan, Turkmenistan, Afghanistan and Pakistan. It is made from a square of fabric with three of its corners folded inwards and their edges sewn together to create a pocket. The fourth corner, which usually has a fastening attached to it, is left loose to form the bag's opening. This simple but flexible design can be easily adapted to incorporate a range of traditional embellishments. These bags are often small, with each side measuring around 40 cm, which means remnants of fabric can be used. The highly skilled seamstresses of the Banjara people adorn their bags with detailed embroidery and shells, while the Maldhari women from Sindh use patchwork techniques to create meticulous geometric patterns.

In the Bhopa Rapari community, any wedding trousseau worthy of the name should include at least five large dowry bags, known as _khotalo_. According to Judy Frater's study of the textiles of nomadic communities, in her book _Threads of Identity_ (1995), each bag is reserved for a specific use: one is used for storing sweets, others for the bride's clothes, her bodices, veils and skirts, and another for the gifts that the groom distributes to guests. Like the _bachakadiyo_, the embellishments on a _khotalo_ reflect the cultural identity and heritage of its creator.

UZBEKISTAN

PATCHWORK HAT & BOOTS

The accessories shown here originate from Central Asia. As can be seen in the painting on p. 8, the Sufi mystics known as dervishes often dress very distinctively, with tall hats and long coats that are sometimes made from a patchwork of fabrics.

These costumes are a way of showing that the dervishes do not care about material wealth and instead choose a life of simplicity. However, their festive garments are nonetheless striking in appearance. This tall hat, with a band of sheepskin around the rim, is made from recycled fabrics: *ikat*-dyed silk, brocade, velvet, woven silk and cotton taken from old clothes, stitched together to form four solid panels that are then quilted. Over the centuries, clothing patched together from remnants has often worn by pilgrims, shamans, monks and dervishes, and is widely seen as a symbol of humility and the decision to eschew worldly luxuries.

These leather-trimmed women's boots from Uzbekistan are a much bolder form of costume. They are made from offcuts of embroidered *suzani* fabric and remnants of patchwork wall hangings. The end result is a pair of soft, flexible boots that are beautifully embellished – ideal for wearing indoors but too lightweight to be worn outside.

Opposite, above left:
Purse (*bachakadiyo*). Cotton, cowrie shells. H. 45 cm, w. 30 cm when opened. Kutch, Gujarat, India. Catherine Legrand Collection.

Opposite, above right:
Purse (*bachakadiyo*). Cotton. H. 30 cm, w. 30 cm. Banjara community. India. Liliane and Armel Chichery Collection.

Opposite, below:
Large dowry bag (*khotalo*). Cotton. H. 90 cm, w. 66 cm. Maldhari community. Sindh, Pakistan. Wahid Wazir Collection.

Above right:
Dervish hat. *Ikat*-dyed silk, brocade, velvet, silk, offcuts of embroidered cotton, fur. H. 28 cm. Uzbekistan. Catherine Legrand Collection.

Below right:
Boots. Leather sole, back and lining. Upper made from a patchwork of embroidered *suzani* fabric and offcuts from wall hangings. H. 35 cm. Uzbekistan. Catherine Legrand Collection.

CAROQ & YURUK YASTIK

In Central Asia, these small square panels, called *caroq*, were once used to decorate the storage bags that hung from the sides of tents or yurts. Since many people in the region no longer live nomadic lives, this function has become obsolete, but the *caroq* have lost none of their charm.

Now used as wall hangings, the *caroq* are made up of many tiny pieces of fabric arranged around a central motif of five diagonally arranged squares surrounded by rows of tiny triangles in an arrow-like pattern, reminiscent of the Flying Geese motif found on British and American quilts. The border of black and white triangles is thought to ward off the evil eye.

The design is made up of an assortment of squares and triangles of varying sizes. *Caroq* are made using traditional patchwork techniques, with pieces stitched into blocks and then strips. Trying to identify the different fabrics among the jumble of scraps and recycled pieces of *camiz* and *chapan* (kaftans) is a fascinating challenge. They include silks of varying quality, both patterned and plain, satins and pieces of *abr* (fabric made from silk and cotton with warp yarns dyed using the *ikat* technique), woven in the Fergana region or Bukhara. Cotton shapes embroidered using couching stitch or chain stitch sit alongside pieces from *suzani* wall hangings and scraps of *gyrmyzy donlyk*, a fabric with fine red, yellow and black stripes, typically used in Turkmen kaftans. There are also pieces of *mashru*, a striped satinweave fabric made from a blend of silk and cotton.

Also included are a few scattered scraps of mass-produced prints from Russia or other former Soviet countries, taken from the linings of coats. White triangles and geometric patterns in black cotton bring out the colours of the silk – shades of raspberry, garnet, burgundy, pink, orange and fuchsia. The silks

naturally shimmer in the light and make the rich reddish hues of the design seem even more vibrant.

According to Susan Meller's book *Silk and Cotton* (2013), it is traditional to incorporate a scrap of clothing that once belonged to a particularly fertile woman or any highly respected person into a *caroq*, so that it will protect the owner against the evil eye. Similar techniques are used to make *yuruk yastik* like the one shown opposite, large patchworks that are used as wall hangings or bedcovers.

Above:
Small wall hangings (*caroq*). Silk and cotton, some *ikat*-dyed or recycled from lining fabric. 82 × 82 cm, 90 × 90 cm and 92 × 92 cm. Uzbekistan, late 20th century. Tuulikki Chompré Collection.

Opposite:
Detail of a *yuruk yastik* wall hanging. Silk, cotton, scraps of *ikat* and printed fabrics. 175 × 145 cm. Uzbekistan, late 20th century. Catherine Legrand Collection.

TURKMENISTAN

ELEK, KIRLIK & CAROQ

The Turkmen people have both Turkish and Iranian ancestry. They were once nomadic but began to settle from the 1920s onwards, when their freedom of movement was restricted, especially by the impact of Soviet collectivization.

In the Ersari community in Turkmenistan, boys and girls up to the age of four or five traditionally wear a tunic called an *elek*, which is often made from pieces of silk or cotton recycled from adult clothing. The fabric may be further adorned with amulets called *doga*, small pieces of stamped metal, and tassels. These talismans, which shift every time the child moves, are designed to ward off the evil eye. Another common feature in children's clothing is the lack of hem on the tunic. It is deliberately left unfinished so that the child has room to grow, which symbolically ensures they will live a long life. This custom was once common in communities where infant mortality rates were high.

This *elek* (opposite below) is a patchwork of different fabrics. There is cotton with a large floral motif, printed in Russia for the Central Asian market, pieces of silk velvet and, on the sleeves, triangular pieces of *alacha*, a handwoven striped fabric often used for adults' kaftans. On either side of the central panel are white stripes adorned with raw-edged appliqué triangles. Two metal buttons, dating back to the former Soviet Union, are attached to the points of the sleeves.

A bib called a *kirlik* (opposite above) is worn over the tunic. This example, with its fancy jagged border, was probably the work of a Turkmen mother from the Yumut community, and includes a whimsical assortment of patches of silk, cotton and wool, with appliqué red triangles and embroidery stitches.

The patchwork kaftan (left), made for a child, is also known as *caroq*, a term that – as Susan Meller notes in her book *Silk and Cotton* (2013) – can refer to both the technique and the garment. The symmetry of this design lends a sense of order to the joyful mix of colours, achieved by combining strips of silk and cotton, both plain and printed, with rows of small black triangles on a white ground. These triangular motifs, which are also found on wall hangings, are believed to ward off bad luck.

ASMALYK

On their wedding day, brides from the Teke people of Turkmenistan traditionally arrive at their new marital home on the back of a Bactrian camel. The camel wears a set of trappings called *asmalyks*, which are specially made for the ceremony, then kept as a memento afterwards.

In this part of Central Asia, where the majority of the population is Muslim, the most important milestones in life are birth, circumcision, marriage, pilgrimage to Mecca and death. There is a ceremony to mark each stage of a person's life, with its own rituals, textiles, clothes and accessories, all of which are imbued with symbolic meanings.

Teke wedding ceremonies are nothing short of spectacular. The bride arrives riding a camel, hidden from the eyes of onlookers in a covered litter positioned between its two humps. Panels of open patchwork are draped over the animal's neck and flanks, while an embroidered hood is placed on its head and ornamental kneepads are fastened to its legs. These patchwork decorations are designed to move with the camel. The *asmalyks*, which are sewn in pairs, are made of rows of squares, stitched corner to corner to form an openwork pattern. Red and green are usually the dominant colours. Each square has a backing, and is sometimes trimmed with braid or embroidery. Locks of children's hair and other talismans may be sewn onto the *asmalyk*. Another embellishment is a small triangle of padded fabric; this is another type of lucky charm, called a *dogha* or a *tumar*. Tassels made from scraps of cloth adorn the lower edge of the *asmalyk*, swaying as the camel walks.

Below:
Camel trapping (*asmalyk*). Plain silk, *ikat*-dyed silk and printed cotton. 106 × 68 cm. Turkmenistan, early 20th century. Tuulikki Chompré Collection.

Opposite:
Detail of a camel trapping (*asmalyk*). 125 × 115 cm. Turkmenistan, early 20th century. Tuulikki Chompré Collection.

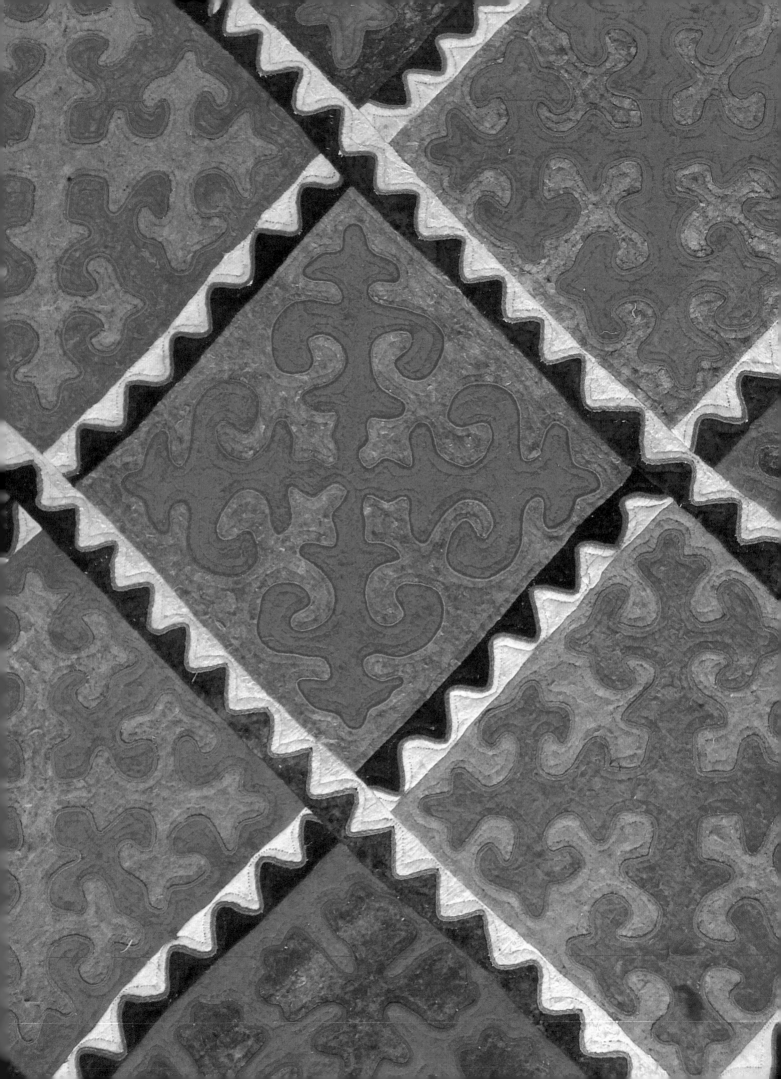

KYRGYZSTAN

KURAK SHYRDAK

Kyrgyzstan is a small republic in Central Asia, formerly part of the Soviet Union. It is home to part of the Tian Shan mountain ranges. For many years, the only fabric available to the Kyrgyz people for making clothes and tents was wool from camels, yaks, sheep and goats.

Traditionally, the Kyrgyz people were farmers who spent the summer months living in yurts made of felt, which remain important symbols of Kyrgyz culture. Felt has many advantages as a fabric: it is environmentally friendly, waterproof, a good insulator of both heat and sound, doesn't tear easily, and after it is cut, the edges can be left raw and will not fray. It is the perfect material for making rugs which, along with wall hangings, form part of a bride's wedding trousseau. In most Kyrgyz homes – whether yurts, apartments or houses – the floors are covered with felt rugs. The *ak-kalpak*, the national hat of Kyrgyzstan, is also made of felt. All of these items are embellished with motifs that are cut out, inserted or appliquéd. The artisans' handiwork is all the more impressive because felt is a tricky fabric to sew.

Making a *kurak shyrdak* rug is a time-consuming process (see p. 13). The first stage involves felting the wool and dyeing it different colours. An easier option is to buy ready-made felt at the market. The seamstress chooses four colours of felt, then cuts out an even number of identical squares, which she places on top of each other and tacks together. She draws lines through the centre of the topmost square – diagonal lines joining the corners and median lines from the midpoints of each edge. Then she uses chalk to draw a motif

in one segment, which is then reflected along these axes. Using a long, sharp blade, she cuts through all the layers at once and slots the cut-out motifs from one colour of felt into the holes in the next layer, so that they interlock. The pieces are then stitched edge to edge, with narrow cord inserted between the colours to create an outline for the motifs. The finished squares are paired up or arranged into larger blocks. In her book *Nomadic Felts* (2011), Stephanie Bunn uses the term 'sister rugs' to describe pairs of rugs where one rug's pattern is the exact inverse of the other. The most common motif is based on a curving ram's horn; in Kyrgyzstan, the ram was historically a symbol of wealth and fertility.

Although this technique may not fit the generally accepted definition of patchwork, it does consist of joining together different fabrics, with special attention to the arrangement of shapes and the combination of colours. The women who sew these rugs are proud of their work and profit from selling their rugs both locally and abroad.

Opposite:
Kurak shyrdak rug (detail). Felted wool. Kyrgyzstan. Catherine Legrand Collection.

Above:
Small hexagonal rug (*kurak shyrdak*), usually placed at the entrance to a yurt. Felted wool. Diameter 70 cm. Kyrgyzstan. Catherine Legrand Collection.

Right:
Kurak shyrdak rug. Felted wool. 90 × 62 cm. Kyrgyzstan. Tuulikki Chompré Collection.

KOREA

HANBOK

Traditional Korean costumes feature an array of delicate and colourful garments and a wealth of subtle details. Colours have symbolic meanings and must be carefully combined in a way that creates harmony. In Korean culture, the universe is symbolically divided into five elements, five cardinal directions and five colours.

Black is seen as cold, fluid and infinite; it is associated with the north, winter, water and wisdom. White stands for the west, autumn, iron, purity, detachment and holiness. Blue represents the east, but also spring, wood, trees, cold and steadfastness. Summer is red, which also stands for the south, fire and good fortune. Finally, yellow is the colour of the emperor: it represents the centre, the earth, authority and wealth.

On Korean ceremonial clothing, these colours often appear in the form of multicoloured sleeves, reminiscent of the wings of exotic birds. On their first birthday, Korean girls and boys traditionally wear a multicoloured jacket (*saekdong jeogori*) or a short coat (*saekdong durumagi*). The body of the garment is usually a single colour, but the sleeves are made up of stripes of fabric in different colours, arranged in a particular order that represents the five cardinal directions and their accompanying virtues: kindness, obedience, courtesy, modesty and humility. These are associated with a good upbringing and were once believed to protect the child against illness.

Festivals, New Year's celebrations and weddings are all opportunities for Koreans to wear their *hanbok*. For women, this costume consists of a *jeogori* – a short jacket with a sash fastening – and a *chima* – a full-length wrap skirt – as well as matching accessories.

The *hanbok* dates back to the Three Kingdoms period, which lasted from 57 BCE to 668 CE, and was widely worn until the 1950s. The sleeves of women's *jeogoris* look as delicate as a butterfly's wings. Both the skirt and the jacket are made from woven ramie fabric, a plant fibre from the nettle family, or from plain silk gauze or silk twill. The colour red is usually reserved for weddings.

Patchwork may be incorporated in two ways: to create the striped sleeves, or as an additional form of embellishment. As the former South Korean Minister of Culture Lee O-young said of the *hanbok* created by the fashion designer Lee Young-hee, 'When I undress, I am in my natural state. When I dress, I am wearing my culture.'

Above:
Child's overcoat with multicoloured sleeves (*saekdong durumagi*). Silk in five colours and silk brocade embellished with Chinese symbols of joy and longevity. This garment is sometimes called a 'magpie coat'; magpies are a symbol of good luck. This *saekdong durumagi* would be worn to a New Year's celebration by a boy (as can be seen from the blue sash) under seven years old. Korea, late 20th century.

Opposite:
Hanbok costume, comprising a jacket and skirt. The jacket (*jeogori*) fastens on the right-hand side with a sash (*goreum*). H. 26 cm, arm span 130 cm. Pleated wrap skirt (*chima*) attached to a high waistband. H. 110 cm. Decorative tassels (*norigae*) hang from jade pendants. The red fabric means that this is a wedding dress. Korea, late 20th century.

BOJAGI

The word *bojagi* is thought to derive from the Chinese word *pojaui*, which means 'clothing for objects'. The name says it all: *bojagi* are square wrapping cloths.

Bojagi can be as small as one *p'ok*, a standard square with sides measuring around 35 cm, or up to ten *p'ok* for wrapping larger items. They have many potential uses; at Korean weddings they are used to wrap the carved ducks or geese traditionally used in the ceremony, to cover the *ham* box, which holds gifts from the groom's family, and to wrap presents. In everyday life, *bojagi* are used to store official documents, cover food and wrap clothing, jewelry and laundry. A *bojagi* is more than just a wrapping; it is a gift in itself. They became less common after the Second World War but are experiencing a modest renaissance, boosted by their environmentally friendly and aesthetic qualities.

The *bojagi* once used at the Imperial court were made from squares of painted or brocaded silk, but it is the everyday *bojagi* – *min-bo* and *chogak-bo* – that are most

interesting. These patchwork *bojagi* are made using *chogak*, small offcuts of fabric left over after making an item of clothing. *Bojagi* are most commonly made from leftover *hanbok* fabric – lightweight silk, silk twill or ramie in various colours.

There are many styles of *bojagi*. Some, like the one pictured opposite, are made up of geometric shapes, with squares, triangles, rectangles and rhomboids arranged in a symmetrical pattern around a central point or axis. The shapes get bigger as they move away from the centre. Other *bojagi* are made from irregular shapes in an apparently random design (see left), resembling a crazy quilt (see p. 70). However, there is nonetheless an order to the composition, with the shapes arranged into square blocks or rows.

Bojagi may be multicoloured or white. Ideally, coloured *bojagi* should include the five auspicious colours (see p. 148) and achieve a balance between yin and yang. The pieces are joined using close overedge stitching that is deliberately left visible. Monochrome *bojagi*, often made from leftover scraps, have no backing fabric, making them translucent. There are also winter *bojagi* made from quilted cotton, and others that are ornately embroidered. The maker cuts out the pieces, leaving a border of a few millimetres, then sews them together using running stitch. The felled seams are visible through the fine fabric, an attractive feature that enhances the graphic feel of the design, which can be viewed from both sides. Whatever the design or fabrics used, the *bojagi* is edged with a border and a fastening is attached, often to one of the corners.

Bojagi occupy a unique place in Korean culture. They are works of art in their own right, their geometric splendour recalling the paintings of Paul Klee or Piet Mondrian.

Opposite:
Wrapping cloth (*bojagi mosi chogakbo*). Monochrome patchwork made of around 200 scraps of ramie fabric. No backing. 115 × 115 cm. Korea, early 20th century. Claire and Pierre Ginioux Collection.

Above:
Wrapping cloth (*bojagi kyoppo*). Multicoloured patchwork with silk organza backing. 39 × 39 cm. Korea, 21st century. Maryse Allard Collection.

JAPAN

MOMPE & FUTONJI

In recent years, Western culture has seen a rise in interest in the Japanese idea of *boro*, which encompasses the ideas of reusing, recycling and degrowth. The principle of *wabi-sabi*, which involves an acceptance of imperfection, ageing and transience, has likewise become better known outside of Japan. This spiritual concept has its roots in Buddhism and Taoism, and brings together the principles of simplicity, modesty and melancholy (*wabi*) with the ideas of damage or wear and tear (*sabi*).

One way in which the philosophy of *wabi-sabi* is applied to the material world is in the art of *kintsugi*, a Japanese method of repairing pottery; instead of disguising mended cracks, artisans use lacquer dusted with powdered gold to highlight the imperfection. This highly skilled technique reflects the concept of *yo no bi*, which means 'beauty in practical objects'. It became popular during the *mingei* folk craft movement that began in the mid-1920s, founded by Yanagi Soetsu, and echoes the philosophy of *wabi-sabi* in its modesty and celebration of decay.

Most makers of *boro* works are far removed from these philosophical and aesthetic theories, but the pieces they create from reused scraps of fabric nevertheless display a clear feel for size, shape, colours, materials and patterns.

The patchwork futon cover (*futonji*) and work trousers (*mompe*) shown here are prime examples of *boro*. The work trousers (above), in a style still worn in rural areas, are made from striped cotton, and the sewn-on patches have been carefully placed to ensure that the stripes all run in the same direction. The futon cover

(opposite), on the other hand, is made from such a miscellaneous collection of fabrics that it almost looks like a swatch book. It is made from five panels, each 32 cm wide, sewn edge to edge. Fabric patches cover the holes but do not hide them, giving the *futonji* a deliberately worn feel.

The fabrics used are a mixture of hemp and cotton, woven cloth that has been dyed indigo, scraps of *ikat* weave (*kasuri*) and double-*ikat* fabric (*tateyoko kasuri*), and striped (*tatejima*) or checked (*kosi moyo*) materials, mostly left over from making clothes. Despite the wide variety of fabrics, the colours provide visual coherence, with the dominant indigo (*aizome*) punctuated by white dots, lines and checks. The layers are held together with large running stitches that form patterns extending across the pieced surface of the fabric, bringing a sense of harmony to the apparently random composition.

Above:
Work trousers (*mompe*) made from reused cotton fabric. H. 85 cm. Japan. Claudine Lachaud Collection.

Opposite:
Detail of futon cover (*futonji*) made from reused fabric. Indigo cotton and *ikat*-dyed cotton. 5 panels, each 32 cm wide. 190 × 156 cm. Tohoku, Japan, mid-20th century. Liliane and Armel Chichery Collection.

Right:
Kimono (*donza-boro*). Plain
cotton and striped woven
cotton. H. 140, w. 65 cm, arm
span 135 cm. Japan, *c.* 1950.
Yves Venot Collection.

*Opposite, from left to right
and top to bottom:*
Bag (*bukuro*) and its lining.
Silk. H. 50 cm. Japan.
Catherine Legrand Collection.

Offering bag (*komebukuro*).
Indigo cotton. H. 35 cm. Japan.
Catherine Legrand Collection.

Woman's bag. *Ikat*-dyed with
appliqué embellishments,
ramie and silk crepe. H. 17 cm,
w. 20 cm. Japan. Liliane and
Armel Chichery Collection.

DONZA-BORO

The patchwork kimono shown opposite looks spectacular, but in fact it is a *donza-boro*, a modest indigo kimono of the kind worn by Japanese farmers and fishermen from the 19th to the early 20th century.

It is made up of scraps of fabric pieced together to cover holes and threadbare areas. The term *boro* is used for any kind of torn or worn-out textiles, including clothing, accessories, throws and bed covers. The *donza* was traditionally worn by farmers from the north of Japan, and includes a layer of batting made from scraps of hemp or cotton to create extra warmth. The fabric from a large kimono can be recycled into *boro* when it is worn out, then may eventually end up as a *yogi*, a kind of quilt in the shape of a kimono that people wrap themselves in to sleep.

BUKURO

These charming, elegant bags illustrated below combine modesty and thriftiness with aesthetic appeal.

The light-coloured bag (top left), called a *bukuro*, is made up of more than forty different pieces of fabric, probably taken from women's kimonos, given that the colours and fabrics are so delicate. Paler strips of silk with tie dye (*shibori*) patterns are interspersed with bands of red silk brocade, resulting in a patchwork rectangle sewn onto a square background. This bag is reversible; its lining (top right) features a different patchwork design. The reason for this is unclear: is it an aesthetic choice, or a practical one motivated by a lack of fabric? Double-sided patchwork can also be found on some Swedish and American quilts. The lining of this bag could easily serve as the exterior, as it is made from silk in muted shades with *ikat* patterns, edged with a band of pale purple.

The indigo bag (bottom left) is made from pieces of *ikat* weave (*kasuri*) and plain fabric. It is called a *komebukuro* (*kome* means 'rice') and is designed to hold offerings of rice and beans, which are given to monasteries. The makers reuse scraps of fabric from worn-out kimonos or old futon covers, piecing them together in a carefully chosen composition. This bag is made up of squares that stand on their corners, each cut from a different fabric.

The small bag with the bird design (bottom right) has a fairytale quality. It is made from a strip of *ikat*-dyed ramie fabric, with appliqué motifs resembling rounded hills, cut from pink and red silk crepe and *ikat*. A small bird made of silk has been appliquéd on one of the hills and embellished with embroidery. The underside of the bag is decorated with a subtle hexagonal patchwork motif.

NORAGI & TATTSUTE

Chuzaburo Tanaka is an important figure in the history of *boro*. Born in 1933 in Aomori prefecture, in the northernmost part of Honshu, he was an archaeologist, ethnographer and collector who specialized in the rural culture of the Tohoku region. Over the course of more than forty years, he built up a vast collection of recycled textiles that included fishermen's kimonos with white decorative stitching (*kogin-zashi*), undergarments (*mataware*) made from reused fabric, workwear kimonos (*noragi*), gaiters and mittens, and an assortment of tattered second-hand clothing and scraps of fabric that he saved before they were reduced to mere shreds. Very much ahead of his time, he was one of the first people to recognize the emotive power of *boro* as a symbol of the rural poverty that was once commonplace in Japan and the spirit of thriftiness practised in many households.

Cotton grown in India, China and Korea was not imported to Japan until a relatively late date. For centuries, it remained a luxury, like silk, and was only worn by the aristocracy. Ordinary Japanese people made fabric from indigenous plants such as hemp, ramie, linden and wisteria, or from *shifu*, recycled paper. Making these fibres into threads for weaving required a great deal of work and the end product was a thin fabric that was better suited to warmer climates than the snowy north of the country. Farmers in central Japan eventually started growing cotton, but this practice never reached the northernmost regions.

The softness, suppleness and rareness of cotton soon made it a sought-after material. A trade in second-hand clothing and textiles sprang up, with goods being transported from south to north by sea, then from 1892 onwards by the Tohoku Railway. Travelling salesmen and peddlers, called *tabeto*, went all over the countryside with bags holding up to 25 kg of cloth. Women would pool their resources to buy a bundle and share the pieces out among themselves before washing and bleaching them with lime. These old cloths, called *tsugi*, were mostly dyed with indigo, either in a block colour, or with stripes or checks. The bundles included pieces of *kasuri* – an *ikat* weave used to make *noragi* and kimonos – as well as pieces of *katazome*, *norizome* and *tsutsugaki*, resist-dyed fabrics that featured white patterns on a coloured ground. Some of the scraps included Japanese characters representing the name of a company or trade association. Even a tiny piece of fabric can reveal a great deal about its geographic origins or local production techniques.

Some lengths of fabric were large enough to make a *noragi* (work jacket) or *sodenashi* (sleeveless jacket), but most were small and were used to patch holes in old clothing. Pieces of various sizes were arranged in an overlapping fashion and sometimes covered the seams of a garment but never changed its basic structure. The patches were sewn on with running stitch; whipstitch was very rarely used. In some cases, it is no longer possible to identify which fabric a piece of clothing was originally made from, as so many patches have been added. Larger pieces of higher-quality fabric (*noshi-tsugi*) were separated from the more tattered scraps (*sakiori*); these were torn into strips, twisted and knotted together to make sleeveless jackets, kimonos or belts (*obi*), following a similar method to the one used for making rag rugs. Rags were also braided to make headbands, worn to absorb sweat.

Opposite, above:
Workwear kimono (*noragi*). Second-hand *ikat*-dyed cotton. Lined and quilted. H. 80 cm, arm span 120 cm. Japan. Catherine Legrand Collection.

Opposite, below:
Work shorts. Second-hand *ikat*-dyed cotton. Unlined. 55 × 55 cm. Japan. Catherine Legrand Collection.

ATTUSH

This vintage postcard from the early 20th century shows an Ainu couple wearing traditional clothing and standing in front of their home. It dates back to a time when the only foreign visitors to the island of Hokkaido, in the north of the Japanese archipelago, were a few ethnographers and the photographers who accompanied them.

The man is wearing a kimono-like garment made of pale cloth, probably woven from nettle fibres, with a band of appliqué motifs around the lower hem. On top of this, he wears a sleeveless jacket made from brown fabric. He has a sword tied at his waist and holds a staff, and he sports the thick beard that was traditional for Ainu men. His wife wears an indigo kimono called a *kaparamip*, made of cloth that was probably imported from Honshu, which is embellished with a broad appliqué design made of beige fabric and embroidered with chain stitch in blue thread. Her hair is partly covered by an indigo headband decorated with a curving arabesque motif. Unlike many Ainu women of this period, she does not have traditional blue lip tattoos.

Although the Ainu people are indigenous to Japan, they share many beliefs with the people who live in the most easterly part of Siberia. Their traditional clothing reflects this dual heritage. The fabric for Ainu kimonos, called *attush*, was usually woven from fibres from the bark of the elm tree (*ohyo*), which is sacred to the Ainu people. The shape resembles the straight lines of a Japanese kimono, but the decorative motifs are similar to those used in Siberia. A maze-like network of strips forms a barrier around the openings of the garment – around the neck and wrists, across the front and around the hem. These motifs, called *kiribuse*, have their roots in shamanic beliefs and were believed to keep evil spirits away. They are always made from fabric in a contrasting colour to the garment itself, creating a striking juxtaposition of shades.

Ainu seamstresses would cut out the appliqué motifs from cotton imported from Honshu and sew them on with small, close stitches, using thread of a similar hue to the fabric. The labyrinthine patterns are symmetrical across the central line of the garment. Embroidery has been used to extend the corners of the strips to form decorative points – a feature that may have its roots in traditional beliefs. The appliqué bands were overstitched with curving lines of chain stitch (*oho*) in a contrasting shade of thread.

Although the cultural traditions of the Ainu are still fiercely protected, these kimonos are no longer worn, but they remain highly sought after by museums and private collectors.

Above:
Vintage postcard. Ainu couple. Hokkaido. Japan, early 20th century.

Opposite:
Front and back views of an Ainu kimono (*attush*). Cloth woven from elm bark fibre, with appliqué motifs and embroidery. H. 118 cm, arm span 118 cm. Hokkaido, Japan, late 19th century. Bruno Lussato Institute, Brussels.

HYAKUTOKU KIMONO

Hyaku is the number 'one hundred' in Japanese, while toku means 'virtues'. A hyakutoku kimono is made up of many different pieces of fabric, each representing a different positive trait.

As mentioned earlier, for a long time cotton was a rare and precious fabric in Japan, especially in the Tohoku region in the north. To celebrate the birth of a child, it was customary for friends and relatives to give the new mother small pieces of fabric as a good-luck charm. The scraps were taken from clothes that had been worn and were therefore believed to be symbolically imbued with the virtues of their former owners. The mother would then use these precious pieces of material to make a small 'hundred virtues' kimono like the one shown here. Although the colour palette of this kimono is mainly dark and subtle, it brings together an appealing variety of fabrics, including block colours, stripes, checks, *ikat*

Opposite and above:
Girl's 'hundred virtues' kimono (*hyakutoku*): rear view (*opposite*) and lining (*above*). Cotton and silk with auspicious symbols on the back. H. 73 cm, arm span 74 cm. Japan, Meiji era (1868–1912). Kazuko Nakano Collection.

weave (*kasuri*), tie-dye (*shibori*) and stencil motifs (*katazome*). At first glance, this 'hundred virtues' kimono may look similar to a *boro* kimono (see p. 154), but on closer inspection it is clear that both the design and the techniques used to make it are very different.

Here, the patches of fabric are arranged in a symmetrical pattern. No overstitching or appliqué is used; instead, the seams that join the pieces together are hidden on the inside. The maker has carefully arranged the pieces so that the two sides reflect each other, and she has alternated the colours and patterns to create striking juxtapositions. Pieces of red fabric, a colour worn only by girls, have been used to make a second patchwork layer that functions as a lining, meaning that the child is doubly protected by two layers of virtue.

Adding together the number of patchwork pieces on both sides makes 197 in total, all for a kimono that measures only 73 by 74 cm, creating a beautiful mosaic.

At a time when infant mortality rates were high, mothers would often take extra precautions to keep their children safe and well, sewing a few threads with protective properties (called *senui*) or a talisman called a *semamori* into the back of the garment. This kimono, from the collection of Kasuko Nakano, is embroidered on the back with a circular motif called *fukura suzume*, which literally means 'a puffed-up sparrow', but also incorporates the characters meaning good luck (*fuku*) and kindness (*ra*).

VIETNAM

FLOWER LOLO COSTUME

This Vietnamese ethnic group are known as the Flower Lolo. However, the patterns on this jacket, trousers and plastron are not floral, but made from a mosaic of small triangles. The jacket boasts more than a thousand pieces of fabric, which together create a dazzling sense of movement that is reminiscent of Op art paintings.

Triangles with sides measuring around 1 cm are appliquéd onto larger triangles using whipstitch. The use of block-colour fabrics, with a heavy emphasis on red, creates a stunning mosaic effect, while the triangular repeat motif gives unity to the whole design. As in much traditional patchwork of this kind, the triangles are paired to form squares, then pieced into larger blocks, before being appliquéd onto the indigo or black cotton that makes up the jacket, trousers and plastron.

Lolo seamstresses sometimes include additional motifs using reverse appliqué. They place two squares of cotton in different colours on top of each other, draw a design on the top square, cut it out, then turn and stitch the cut edges. The colour of the square beneath shows through, creating a reversed-out pattern. Nowadays, some Lolo costumes are made from black synthetic velvet rather than indigo cotton, and adorned with a scattering of plastic sequins, proving how even traditional garments can evolve over time.

Today, it is rare to see people wearing these costumes, as most Lolo women favour casual Western-style clothes. On a visit to Sang Pa'a, I was lucky enough to persuade two young village women to take their traditional costumes out of the chests in which they were stored and put them on. One explained: 'My mother gave me this outfit when I got married. I don't wear it now as I don't want to damage it. I wouldn't be able to sew it myself, it's too much work, too complicated.'

The Lolo community belongs to the Sino-Tibetan group of peoples. There are about 4,000 Lolo people in Vietnam. The Flower Lolo live in the Meo Vac district along the Chinese border, while the Black Lolo live in the province of Cao Bang, within Vietnam, and many Lolo people also live on the other side of the border in Yunnan.

Left:
Two Lolo women in Sang Pa'a, close to the Vietnam–China border.

Above and opposite (detail):
Traditional women's costume of the Flower Lolo people. Cotton. Jacket: h. 45 cm, arm span 127 cm. Plastron: h. 97 cm, w. 67 cm. Trousers: h. 80 cm. Meo Vac region, Vietnam, late 20th century. Catherine Legrand Collection.

SUA HII

The Tai people includes many different groups spread across China, Vietnam, Laos and Thailand, all descended from speakers of the Tai language. They should not be confused with the Thai people – citizens of Thailand – although some Tai people are also Thai.

This black cotton tunic, called a *sua hii*, is traditionally worn by women from the White Tai community in Son La province of northwest Vietnam. Although the Tai community are famed for their weaving, there are only a few sections of woven fabric on this tunic, aside from the decorative collar and band around the hem. The tunic is embellished with appliquéd vertical stripes cut from mass-produced cotton in a variety of block colours, arranged in a deliberately asymmetrical manner. The stripes are simply stitched in place, but this does not lessen their visual impact. They give the tunic a very contemporary feel and provide a bold contrast with the base fabric, which is always dark, either indigo or black. They also highlight the structure of the tunic, which is made from a narrow length of fabric material only 35 cm wide, by covering the seams that connect the different parts: front, back, side panels, shoulders and sleeves.

Many items of traditional clothing worn by different ethnic communities feature bands of embroidery, braid or appliqué, which are used to highlight, reinforce or simply embellish the seams. These additions are a useful way to strengthen parts of the garment that are softer or may wear out more quickly, such as the shoulder seams, cuffs and hem.

As in the traditional costumes of the Ainu people of Japan (see p. 158), these stripes and adornments were originally intended to offer symbolic protection, preventing evil spirits called *phi* from entering the body. The Tai long believed that *phi* were responsible for diseases and disasters. When a woman from the White Tai community dies, she is laid to rest with her *sua hii* spread out over her coffin, with the embellished side facing down so that it can continue to protect her in the next world.

Below:
Tunic (*sua hii*) of the White Tai people. Cotton with silk appliqué. 125 × 110 cm. Son La province, Vietnam. Liliane and Armel Chichery Collection.

LAOS

AKHA TRADITIONAL DRESS

The cultures of minority communities in southeast Asia are often threatened by integration and assimilation, with age-old customs and traditional knowledge at risk of being lost forever. However, the Akha people are particularly determined to keep their culture alive, and their traditional costume is a symbol of this resistance.

The Akha people are spread across several countries – Myanmar, the Yunnan region of China, northern Thailand and Laos – but many Akha communities have been pushed back into mountainous regions and given arid land that is difficult to farm. Visiting the villages in

Above:
Akha costume. Jacket, pleated skirt, plastron with beaded fringe, leg gaiters. Locally woven and mass-produced cotton. Glass beads, shells, pieces of metal. Jacket: 42 × 47 cm. Skirt: h. 33 cm. Leg gaiters: 23 × 14 cm. Muang Sing region, Laos. Catherine Legrand Collection.

the Muang Sing region of northern Laos, it is surprising to see the extent to which Akha customs and traditional dress have survived despite this hostile environment. Although Akha women do not always wear the full traditional outfit on an everyday basis – for example, one woman might choose a tied headscarf instead of the traditional headdress, while another may swap a T-shirt for the jacket – they nonetheless celebrate their culture through their garments.

Although there are as many variations as there are groups and sub-groups, a traditional Akha costume usually includes a jacket (*pehong*), a blouse (*lasha*), a short pleated skirt (*peedee*), a beaded plastron, a pair of leg gaiters (*cubang*) and a bag. There are no restrictions when it comes to embellishing the outfit and the impressive matching headdress. Akha women use a range of embroidery stitches, patchwork motifs, appliqué designs, shells, dried seeds, glass or plastic beads, buttons, old coins, small metal balls, tassels, feathers, and even monkey fur, to enliven the indigo-dyed base fabric.

Over time, Akha women have moved away from making their appliqué decorations from locally woven and dyed cotton and hemp, in favour of mass-produced cotton bought at the market, but the traditional motifs live on. Braids are couched over side seams, appliqué motifs are stitched around cuffs, and leg gaiters are adorned with colourful patches of fabric. Rows of multicoloured cross-stitch motifs alternate with straight or jagged lines in bold shades. The jacket cuffs include reverse appliqué panels, with the blue outer layer cut away to reveal red and white fabric beneath.

VIETNAM & LAOS

LÜ TRADITIONAL DRESS

The two jackets shown here are worn by women from the same ethnic group who live on opposite sides of the Vietnam–Laos border. The jacket on the right belongs to a Lü woman from the region of Phongsali in northern Laos, while the one shown opposite belongs to a Lü woman from Na Tam, a small village in the limestone hills near Lai Chau in northern Vietnam.

The high craggy landscape of northern Laos and Vietnam, along the borders with China and Myanmar, is home to many minority communities. These people have preserved their own languages, customs, religious practices and traditional garments as markers of cultural identity, allowing them to recognize each other and differentiate themselves from the Lao and Kinh majorities. Traditional dress tends to play a more important role for women than for men. Local women are also the ones who weave hemp, raise silkworms, tend to the vats of indigo dye, design resist-dye motifs, and embroider and sew trousers, skirts, tunics, plastrons, leg gaiters, headdresses, bags, hats and children's clothes. These skills, passed down through the generations from mother to daughter, have to some extent proved impervious to the encroachment of modern life, surviving partly thanks to these communities' geographic isolation.

Traditional Lü costumes for women are designed to fit the figure closely. The jacket has a wrap front, forming a high neckline, and the fabric is nipped in at the waist before flaring

out into a peplum around the hips. There are no darts around the bust. The jacket is worn over a sarong or a straight skirt, creating an elegant silhouette.

The jacket from Laos is made from black cotton satin and embellished with a patchwork of narrow multicoloured stripes, each one around 1 cm wide, sewn edge to edge. They snake across the jacket in an elegant curve that follows the line of the hem, forming a kind of rainbow. The simple adornments could be a sign of modest means, or an aesthetic choice, or perhaps some embellishments have been removed. The third possibility seems most likely, since when Lü women have to part with a piece of clothing, they generally remove the silver coins so that they can be kept or sold separately.

Above:
Lü jacket. Cotton satin with appliqué cotton stripes. H. 50 cm, arm span 130 cm. Phongsali province, Laos. Catherine Legrand Collection.

Opposite:
Lü jacket and skirt. Hemp and cotton, printed fabric, pieces of metal, glass beads. Jacket: h. 60 cm, arm span 120 cm. Skirt: 90 × 57 cm. Lai Chau province, Vietnam. Catherine Legrand Collection.

Overleaf, left:
Detail of Lü skirt, incorporating strips of mass-produced cotton fabrics.

Overleaf, right:
Detail of Lü jacket.

The Vietnamese jacket, on the other hand, is lavishly embellished. Although the cut is identical, this jacket is made from hemp and sumptuously decorated with coins dating back to the Chinese colonial era, pieces of stamped metal, spangles and sequins. These glittering metallic adornments are accompanied by a sinuous band of patchwork that wraps around the waist, the neckline and the small of the back. The fabrics are mass-market cotton prints, add a burst of colour to the indigo ground. The collar is decorated with a row of small patchwork squares standing on their corners, while the matching narrow skirt features a patchwork panel made from vertical bands of floral fabric, edged on both sides by a row of tiny appliqué triangles.

VIETNAM & CHINA

CHILDREN'S HATS

Mothers in Vietnam and China traditionally cover their babies' heads from birth because of an ancient belief that this will stop the child's soul from escaping. For the first few years of their life, both girls and boys often wear a snug-fitting cap, which also offers protection from bad weather, bumps and falls.

When a child takes their first steps, it is customary to place a small amount of rice in their hat as a sign of blessing. Around the age of four or five, children stop wearing hats as they are no longer considered to be vulnerable to evil spirits, and – more prosaically – to childhood illnesses. However, out of superstition or nostalgia, many mothers keep these hats for years.

A huge amount of love goes into making these little hats, but very little fabric. A few scraps of cotton, some small pieces of silk, threads, wool and a few small glass beads are all that is needed. To make the hat, a circle of fabric is cut into eight or ten sections, with slightly curved edges to accommodate the rounded shape of the baby's head. The tips of the sections are sewn together, then a twisted knot of fabric is added to form a bobble on top. A rectangular band of cloth forms the rim and is embellished with decorative motifs. Each panel is laid out flat and decorated individually before being sewn to the others. Stars and fiddlehead ferns are some of the most commonly used motifs that are thought to bring good luck, and may be created using patchwork, appliqué or reverse appliqué. Details are outlined with narrow braid, held in place with tiny embroidery stitches. The choice of colours is bold and usually alternated for maximum impact. Embellishments vary from one community to the next and act as symbols of cultural belonging.

The tiger hat (left), with its sharp fangs, bulging eyes, pricked-up ears and long whiskers, is poised to attack any evil spirits that come too close to the baby. A spider embroidered onto its nose is ready to lend a helping hand. A long flap of fabric at the back protects the nape of the neck, considered to be one of the most vulnerable parts of the body. It was believed that a child wearing a *hutoumao* like this one not only benefited from the tiger's protection, but also absorbed its strength and courage. The process of making this delightful piece involved many stages. The ears, eyes, eyebrows and nose were all cut out separately, sewn, embroidered, then appliquéd onto a base that was stiffened with rice starch. This kind of hat is popular among the Han Chinese, but is also worn by babies from the minority peoples living in the southwestern provinces of China.

Opposite:
Children's hats. Cotton, pieces of metal, woollen tassels. Diameter 14 to 16 cm. China and Vietnam. Liliane and Armel Chichery Collection.

Above:
Child's tiger hat (*hutoumao*). Silk and other materials. H. 26 cm, w. 22 cm. China. Catherine Legrand Collection.

HMONG AND MIAO COLLARS & BELTS

The appliqué and reverse appliqué techniques illustrated here are practised by many ethnic groups living along the border between China and Vietnam.

Reverse appliqué is a popular technique among the Miao women of China and their Vietnamese neighbours, the Hmong people. It can be used to embellish all sorts of items: from children's hats (like those shown on the previous page) and bibs to the collar of a tunic or the front of a plastron. Seamstresses often embellish their appliqué with embroidery stitches. Anything goes as long as it allows them to achieve their aim of creating a beautiful garment that celebrates their cultural identity. This heritage is often expressed in surprising forms, such as the delicate detachable collars that Hmong women wear with their tunics. Creating the intricate cut-out patterns in reverse appliqué requires a great deal of skill but only a small amount of fabric. These miniature works of art are also practical; women can stash them in their bags and pull them out whenever they have a free moment to sew. The collars are removed from tunics before washing, to ensure that the indigo dye doesn't run into the delicate fabric; they can also be sewn onto a new garment when the old one wears out. The colour combinations are always complementary, the shapes pleasing, and the handiwork subtle.

Reverse appliqué can be used to create straight lines or voluptuous curves, stepped motifs or stars, chequerboards or Greek keys. Spirals are another popular motif, symbolizing infinity and eternity. The different textiles shown here reflect the diversity of the various communities that created them.

A selection of rectangular collar pieces and motifs used to decorate plastron straps. Reverse appliqué. Vietnamese Hmong and Chinese Miao communities. Catherine Legrand Collection.

CHINA

HEZHE TRADITIONAL DRESS

In ancient Chinese tales, the Hezhe were known by the name Yupi Dazi, meaning 'Fish-Skin Tartars'. The Hezhe of Manchuria are one of fifty-six recognized minority peoples in China. Neighbouring groups, which include the Evenks and the Nanai, are Russian, while the Ainu, who lived on the nearby island of Sakhalin shortly before it became a Russian territory, are Japanese. Together, they make up the indigenous peoples of eastern Siberia.

Living on the banks of the Amur River or the Sea of Okhotsk, the Hezhe were traditionally fishermen and farmers. They were animists who practised shamanic rituals. Their traditional clothing was made from dried fish skin in summer and furs in winter, acting as a symbolic expression of the interdependency between the human world, the animal world and the environment.

The outfit shown here is a fascinating example of how different cultures can come together through textiles. The short high collar, the central front opening, the band of fabric behind the fastenings, the side vents and the five pairs of knotted buttons and loops all identify this jacket as a *tangzhuang*, a costume from the Tang dynasty (618–907 CE). However, the ensemble is not made from indigo cloth but from fish skins – forty for the jacket and twenty-eight for the trousers. It is a practical, unisex outfit that is lightweight but hardwearing and waterproof, a successful combination of cut and fabric, a meeting of two cultures. The lower hems of the trousers and jacket, as well as the cuffs, are embellished with arabesque patterns. In line with the beliefs shared by many communities in eastern Siberia, these embellishments were placed around the openings of the garment to form a barrier to keep out evil spirits.

In eastern Siberia, including among the Hezhe people, it was the men who fished, catching salmon, carp, pike, catfish, trout, sturgeon and kaluga. Every part of the fish was used – whether to provide food for people and their dogs, or to make tents, tarpaulins, clothing, bags, children's toys and talismans.

It was the women's job to gut and wash the fish, remove the fat, cut up the flesh, dry it, clean the skins and sew them together. As soon as young women reached their teenage years, they began to learn these skills from their mothers. Because the fish skins were fairly small, the women had to sew lots of them together to make garments. Patchwork was therefore a necessary skill, but it was nonetheless done with great care. Women chose the best type of fish skin for each garment and arranged the pieces in a symmetrical pattern, paying attention to the grey or amber hues as well as the direction of the scales. The pieces were stitched together with thin strips of stretched fish skin and embellishments were attached using fish glue.

The boots shown above are each made up of four pieces, cut from similar fish skins. As was customary, the sole is made from skin with large scales, aligned so that it grips the slippery ground when the wearer is walking. The cuffs of the boots are decorated with traditional scroll motifs, which were believed to protect the wearer from spirits.

Opposite and above:
Jacket, trousers and boots. Fish leather. Jacket h. 63 × w. 60 cm, arm span 130 cm. Trousers h. 89 cm, waistband 90 cm. Boots h. 24 cm, w. 25 cm. Hezhe people. Manchuria, China. Claire and Pierre Ginioux Collection.

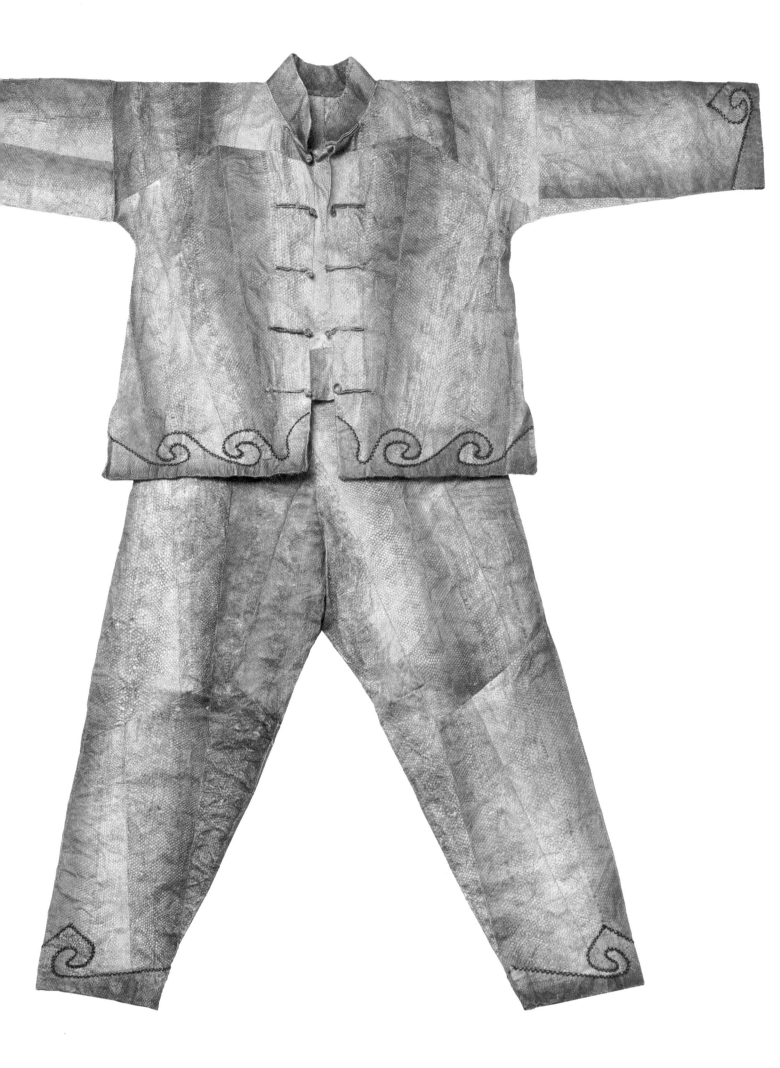

GEJIA BABY CARRIER

Muddy paths and steep mountainsides make it impractical to push a baby around in a pram or stroller. This means that many Chinese mothers from a variety of communities often choose to carry their babies on their backs instead.

Babies tied to their mothers' backs are a common sight in the rice fields, although they can also be seen being carried by their grandmothers or by their older sisters, put in charge of looking after their younger siblings. Ethnic minority groups living in southern China are exempt from the one-child policy that was introduced for the Han majority in 1980, although this policy has recently been relaxed for the Han Chinese as well. This means families may have two or three children, who are often looked after by grandparents while their parents work, sometimes in larger towns and cities a great distance away.

This baby carrier, believed to have been made by the Gejia people, is basically a rectangle of cloth with two long straps. These go over the mother's shoulders, across her chest and then behind her back again, under the baby's bottom, before being tied in front, around her waist. In her book on the textile collection of Philippe Fatin, *Les Chants du fil* (2016), expert in Chinese culture Laure Ozanon gives two reasons why baby carriers acquired from Gejia women are often missing these long straps: either the mother cut them like an umbilical cord when her baby became independent, or she cut them off when she decided to sell the baby carrier and kept them for sentimental or superstitious reasons.

The solid section of the baby carrier is covered with tiny black and white triangles, forming a scale-like pattern. This isn't technically a patchwork technique, as the triangles are made by folding. Small pieces only a few millimetres wide are cut from fabric that has been painted with starch to stiffen it, then they are carefully folded with a fingernail, laid on top of the base fabric and sewn on. The overlapping scales are embellished with sequins and tiny embroidery stitches in different colours. This glittering mosaic is then set inside a border made from indigo cloth.

Above:
Young mother from the Shui community, carrying her baby on her back in a traditional carrier. Guizhou, China.

Below and opposite (detail):
Baby carrier. Cotton and silk. H. 65 cm, w. 43 cm. Gejia people. Guizhou, China. Tuulikki Chompré Collection.

MIAO BABY CARRIER

Young, unmarried women from the Miao community – especially those from the Zhijin region – make their own baby carriers and wear them to festivals and celebrations as a clear statement of intent to young single men.

Some women put a lot of work into making a baby carrier for their future child, while others inherit the one in which their own mother carried them. The carrier has to be both sturdy and beautiful. It is made from a T-shaped piece of fabric with two long straps and is divided into two parts: a stiff back to support the baby and a more flexible seat for under the bottom.

Embroidery, appliqué, inlay, beads and bells – no embellishment is too ornate. The women compete with each other to be the most creative and invent new ways to decorate the baby carriers, aware that they will be judged by them. It is not uncommon to see a baby dozing in a sumptuously decorated carrier, while their father or mother is simply dressed in a T-shirt and jeans. Baby carriers and headdresses are often the last remaining signs of a form of traditional dress that is slowly disappearing.

The baby carrier shown here is distinctive for its decorative relief work. The patterns are cut out from thick, rough twill that is dyed in two different shades of indigo, then appliquéd onto a background of red corduroy. The motifs – peonies and butterflies – are rendered in relief like the patterns on a candlewick bedspread. With its chevron weave, twill stretches on the bias, which makes it easier to add these lightly padded embellishments.

Four stylized bat motifs are arranged around a central circle, with snakes and dragons forming a sinuous border that winds around the edge of the fabric. Bats, which can live up to forty years, are a common symbol of long life in Chinese mythology and are thought to bring good luck to the baby.

Opposite and right (detail):
Baby carrier. Cotton, cotton velvet and silk. Embroidery. 98 × 60 cm. Miao people. Guizhou, China. Catherine Legrand Collection.

Far right:
A grandmother carrying her sleeping grandson in a baby carrier. Guizhou, China.

BABY TROUSERS AND PINAFORE BIB

These miniature trousers have no seat, leaving the infant's bottom bare. The pinafore bib ties around the waist. These charming clothes are so pretty, they seem to have been designed for well-behaved toddlers who never make a mess or go splashing through muddy puddles.

The ingenious pinafore bib (below left) buttons around the baby's neck. It is made from cotton dyed with indigo, a plant-based dye that is known for its insecticide properties. The bat – a symbol of long life, as seen on the Miao baby carrier on the previous page – occupies pride of place in the centre of the appliqué design, surrounded by clouds and spirals.

The other bibs shown here are embellished in a similar fashion: pale blue appliqué on a dark indigo ground, or dark motifs on a light blue ground. The fabric used to make the arabesque patterns is first starched and calendered (pressed, between rollers or traditionally under a large stone) to make it easier to cut and ensure that it doesn't fray. The simplest way to create a symmetrical pattern is to fold the fabric in half, draw the design on one side and cut through both layers, then unfold it. More intricate cut-out patterns are sketched or stamped onto paper, which is then pasted to the reverse side of the fabric, where it serves as both a template and a bonded interfacing that strengthens the delicate cut-out. The motif is then tacked onto the pinafore and secured with satin stitch or couching. The maker uses silk thread or outlines the design with braid or decorative brass wire. Sometimes metallic braid is made by local craftsmen from twisted wire thread.

The trousers shown above reach above the waist and are secured with ties. The sturdy little boots are decorated with appliqué motifs. The soles are made from layers of hemp stitched together, in a similar fashion to the way slippers are often made. As is traditional in much of China, the trousers have no seat – a feature that is still useful today, as it allows parents to easily change disposable nappies.

Left:
Baby trousers. Cotton. H. 50 cm. Dong people. Guizhou, China. Catherine Legrand Collection.

Below:
Pinafore bibs. Cotton. H. 53 cm, w. 36 cm. Miao and Dong people. Guizhou, China. Liliane and Armel Chichery Collection.

Opposite:
Detail of a pinafore bib. Calendered indigo cloth in different shades of blue. Motifs edged with brass metallic braid. Guizhou, China. Amit Zadok Collection.

SHUI WEDDING QUILT

The many festivals of the lunar calendar provide an opportunity for young people from the Shui community to don their finest outfits and meet others from neighbouring villages, play music, drink, laugh and sing duets, as a sign that a young man and woman like each other.

The young man then sends a representative to 'stifle the wind', a phrase that means expressing his desire to marry the girl and getting her family's approval. In her book *La Mosaïque des minorités* (2005), Françoise Grenot-Wang outlines in detail the customs that govern courting and marriage among the minority peoples of southern China. Wedding quilts form part of the bride's trousseau, which she makes herself. They are small and designed for beauty, rather than for warmth. However, not all are indigo dyed or made from patchwork like the one shown here.

This quilt is made up of thirty-five blocks in total. Seven of these are made up of nine smaller squares, each one further divided into triangles. These boldly geometric blocks provide a stark contrast to the rest of the quilt, which is dominated by curved appliqué motifs on an off-white ground. Multiple shades of indigo – from the palest pastel to the darkest, deepest blues – create an elegant effect. The maker collects the pieces of fabric and sorts them according to shade before she starts sewing the quilt.

Many of the blocks are made from four squares sewn together to form a flower motif. When this is repeated, it create a mosaic effect reminiscent of ceramic tiles. The circular motifs are cut out with the aid of a paper template that the maker pastes onto the fabric. The edges are left unturned. Glue made from diluted sticky rice flour is daubed onto the reverse side to reinforce the fabric. The curved designs are outlined with sewn-on braid.

The reverse side of the quilt is almost as attractive as the front. A closer look reveals that each individual square is edged with a narrow border of off-white fabric, and sewn edge to edge with the other blocks with fine overstitching. The quilt is finished with a broad border of dark indigo fabric.

Above:
Shui wedding quilt. Indigo-dyed cotton, approx. 155 × 120 cm. Shui people. Guizhou, China, early 20th century. Galerie Mingei, Paris.

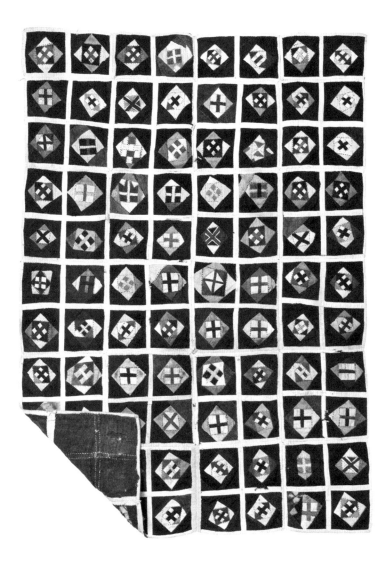

CHINA

MIAO WEDDING QUILT

Xiapei is an important tradition in Miao village life. It is a period when young men are allowed to spend time with girls their own age, to joke around, sing, and form romantic relationships. It is therefore a chance for a young man to choose his bride, or for her to choose him. The groom does not usually need to ask his bride's parents for consent, especially if the woman he wishes to marry comes from the same community.

Above and overleaf (detail):
Miao wedding quilt. Cotton dyed with indigo and other plant-based dyes. 112 × 82 cm. Miao people. Guizhou, China. Catherine Legrand Collection.

In rural China, wedding ceremonies are generally held after the growing season, in the time between the autumn harvests and the New Year's celebrations. Marriage is an important stage of life and young women traditionally prepare for it by making a trousseau to bring with them to their new home. This includes a wedding quilt, a suit for their future husband, gifts for their in-laws and embroidered cloths, as well as a baby carrier that will hold their future children (see pp. 176–179). They give these items to their own mother to look after carefully until their wedding day, or until they give birth to their first child, at which point their handiwork is shown to their in-laws as proof of their talent with the needle.

The inventive geometric patterns and spontaneous feel of this Miao wedding quilt mean it has a similar aesthetic to some African American quilts (see p. 74). It is made up of eighty-eight blocks, each with sides measuring 10 cm. Each square block is embellished with a similar motif and yet each one is individual. A dark indigo cross divides the central square into four sections; this square is surrounded by a larger square on its corner, then another, and so on. Each motif has a slightly uneven quality that adds to its charm. Splashes of faded red, ochre and dusky pink add cheerful touches of colour to this design dominated by off-white and dark indigo. Some of the triangles have been added using appliqué, others with internal seams – both techniques are used interchangeably. The squares are assembled in blocks of four, which are then sewn together. The band of indigo fabric that once formed a border has been removed from this quilt and reused elsewhere.

LUO SKIRT FROM MALIPO

The Malipo region lies in the southeast of Yunnan province, near to Guangxi and just a few miles from the Vietnamese border. The Chinese government considers the Luo community who live in the region to be a subgroup of the Yi people, one of the largest of the fifty-six ethnic minority groups recognized by the People's Republic of China.

The Luo or Lolo people were once called by the name *luóluó*, meaning 'naked.' Now considered pejorative, this term is doubly inappropriate given their elegant traditional dress. The best place to admire the beauty of Luo costumes is a festival that brings the Luo community together every year, held on the first 'Dragon Day' of the first month in the Chinese lunar calendar. At the festival, men and women both wear indigo tunics or jackets embellished with batik motifs and fastened with ties and round silver buttons.

Unlike those of other ethnic groups, the skirts worn by Luo women are gathered rather than pleated. They are not wrap skirts, but are sewn closed with a seam. Slightly less full than those worn by other communities, the skirts are made from two panels of indigo cotton laid out horizontally and gathered into an indigo waistband, creating broad folds in the fabric. The skirt and the matching jacket are embellished with motifs created using wax-resist dyeing (see p. 195).

Strips of fabric decorated with a network of intricate resist-dyed motifs in white and blue alternate with bands of plain indigo. Coloured triangles of fabric are then arranged in pairs to form squares, then sewn onto the plain indigo sections of the skirt to form two bands. The visual effect is not one of uniformity; instead the triangles appear to be scattered at random, interspersed with darker squares that create an irregular rhythm. The triangles are made from cottons, silks or synthetics, stitched together on the reverse or appliquéd. Added lengths of braid and intricate embroidery stitches complement and emphasize the dyed motifs.

Above and opposite (detail): Skirt in cotton, silk, synthetic fabrics. H. 90 cm, w. 160 cm. Luo people. Malipo, China. Liliane and Armel Chichery Collection.

ZHUANG JACKET

'Stay unique, stay Zhuang': these are the words that the Zhuang people have lived by since the 1st century CE. The Zhuang community have lived in China since the paleolithic age. In recent years, they have gained a measure of increased independence, and since 1958, their homeland, the province of Guangxi, has been officially known as the Guangxi Zhuang Autonomous Region.

Zhuang women's traditional clothing consists of a fitted jacket and a long, pleated skirt, both made of indigo-dyed fabric. Looking at this striking jacket, it is hard to tell whether its maker was motivated by thriftiness or simply by creativity.

The jacket is made up of many different fabrics, including around twenty rectangles, ten of which have been cut out from light indigo fabric, and the others from dark indigo. The shade of blue depends on how many times the fabric has been soaked in the vat of indigo dye. Between each soaking, the cloth – at first greenish in colour – is dried and aired out, turning blue on contact with the oxygen in the air. Three or four immersions are enough to dye the material light blue, while a piece of cloth will need to be soaked more than ten times to achieve a dark blue, almost black colour. The fabrics used to make this jacket have been calendered (pressed), which is what gives them their glossy finish. This technique, long associated with indigo, is widely used by minority communities across China.

The Chinese word for indigo is *landian*. Various species of plant that can be used to make indigo dye are grown across southern China, depending on the region, climate and altitude. Species including dyer's knotweed (*Isatis tinctoria*), Chinese indigo (*Polygonum tinctorium*), true indigo (*Indigofera tinctoria*) and Assam indigo (*Strobilanthes cusia*) can be widely found in local vegetable gardens or planted in the shade created by maize crops. The young plants, grown from seedlings, are planted out in the spring, then there are multiple harvests throughout the summer. The leaves and stems are left to steep in a vat of water, for as long as it takes for the fermentation process to be completed. Technically speaking, this means that the indicant in the leaves is hydrolysed. Once this has happened, the leaves are separated out, leaving only the liquid, which is now green. This is vigorously whisked to oxygenate it, until a muddy blue sediment called indoxyl begins to form at the bottom of the vat. The water is then drained, leaving behind a slightly greasy blue paste, which has a very distinctive smell. This valuable dye is collected, wrapped in plastic wrap, stored in large baskets and sold by weight at markets across southeastern China.

Zhuang jacket: front and rear views. Patchwork of calendered indigo cotton in two different shades. Lining in indigo cotton. Asymmetric cut with peplum. Fastened with ties at the underarm. Small side splits, cuffs and collar embellished with strips of woven fabric and embroidery. H. 53 cm, arm span 131 cm. Guangxi, China. Catherine Legrand Collection.

'SKIRT OF A HUNDRED FOLDS'

The Miao women of Yarong and Duncao wear long, elaborate skirts, as do their neighbours, the Buyi people. The story goes that an old Miao woman was first inspired to pleat her skirt by looking at the radiating gills of a large mushroom. Among the ethnic minorities living in southeastern China, there are as many styles of pleated skirts as there are villages. They are explored in greater depth in Catherine Bourzat's book *Les Chants du fil* (2016).

They are known as 'skirts of a hundred folds' but they often have as many as five hundred pleats and may incorporate up to 5 metres of fabric. They are usually wrapped around the waist so that the two edges overlap, with the front opening generally hidden by an apron. The skirts come in a range of lengths, from short ones that wrap around the body three or four times, to full-length styles like those worn by women of the Buyi, Zhuang and Yi communities.

Each community has its own pleating technique. The Dong people use very glossy fabric stiffened by starching and pressing. This process, called 'calendering', flattens the fibres and stiffens the fabric, making it easier to fold. The fabric is laid out on a board, then the pleats are created one by one by pinching the material between the thumb and index finger.

Other communities steam the fabric to fix the pleats in place. They pleat the skirt by hand, starch and press it, then roll it around a bamboo pole and tie it in place. This pole is inserted inside a second bamboo pole with a slightly larger diameter. The skirt, wedged between the two layers of bamboo, is then placed above a source of steam for an hour.

Some makers, like the women of the Buyi and Miao communities in Yarong and Duncao, use a circular pleating technique. They create the pleats by laying the fabric over a barrel or basket that has been specially woven for this purpose. The pleats are all folded in the same direction and tied in place, sprinkled with water containing rice starch, then dried. The seamstress adds parallel lines of stitching to hold the pleats in place.

The long, full skirts made by the Miao women in Duncao and Yarong (see above) are sewn from coarse fabric dyed with indigo. A single panel, 30 cm wide, runs around the waist, then a second panel around 40 cm wide

Above and opposite (detail): Pleated skirt from Yarong. 38 panels. Calendered cotton in two shades of indigo. Striped fabric. Resist-dyed motifs. Braid. Silk thread embroidery. Patchwork and reverse appliqué. H. 70 cm, w. 500 cm. Miao people. Yarong, Guizhou, China. Claire and Pierre Ginioux Collection.

is added below. All of the embellishments are concentrated on this lower section.

The skirts worn by the Miao women in Yarong are a medley of different patterns: rows of striped fabric, bands of patchwork, squares made from two or four triangles placed together, panels of cut-out motifs sewn on using couching stitch, batik panels, appliqué panels made up of triangles sewn on in couching stitch, woven braids and sections of block-colour fabric. All the patterns are beautifully combined, with touches of white, contrasting colours and different shades of indigo. Natural colours – browns, beiges and sandy hues, probably achieved using plant-based dyes – complement the pale blues and dark indigo. Curved motifs are combined with stripes, creating a harmonious balance between the proliferating patterns.

The skirt shown above, made by a Miao woman in Duncao, is equally impressive. It is constructed in the same way, is the same width, uses a similar colour palette and features a similar combination of motifs and stripes, yet the effect is completely different.

At first glance, part of the skirt looks as if it's been made from a band of fabric printed with small motifs, but in fact this is a long patchwork section, made up of more than three hundred squares, each with 6 cm sides, stitched together on the reverse. Each square is embellished with T-shaped motifs in groups of two or four. Each of the smaller T-shapes is cut out from a square of indigo fabric, allowing the brown fabric behind to show through, then edged with couching. The larger T-shapes are cut out from beige or blue fabric, then appliquéd onto an indigo square, edged with couching and embroidered with tiny diamond shapes. The squares are alternated, forming an intricate mosaic, but if the T-shaped motifs have any significance, it remains mysterious.

Above and opposite (detail):
Pleated skirt from Duncao.
Indigo cotton, striped fabric.
Patchwork, appliqué and
reverse appliqué. H. 70 cm,
full width 500 cm. Miao
people. Duncao, Guizhou,
China. Liliane and Armel
Chichery Collection.

GREEN MIAO SKIRT

Villages such as Guizhong, home to the Green Miao people, are built on the craggy mountainsides of Guizhou. The local women traditionally wear pleated skirts that come down to their knees, short jackets, aprons and gaiters to protect their legs. The pleated skirts flutter as the women come and go, carrying yokes across their shoulders.

This skirt is made up of twenty-seven panels of cotton. Each piece is 36 cm long – the full width of the fabric it is cut from, with the selvedge used as a hem. There are fourteen sections decorated with resist-dyed patterns, separated by thirteen strips of plain fabric. Sitting under an awning, with a rectangle of white fabric spread out on a board in front of her, the dyer drips on hot wax to create stripes, friezes, squares, diamond shapes and Greek keys. The denser a pattern is, and the more fabric it covers, the paler in colour the skirt will be, as the wax forms a seal that stops the indigo dye from soaking into the cloth. The fabric is soaked multiple times in a vat of indigo dye, then the wax is removed by soaking it in boiling water. The fabric is then rinsed and dried, ready for the next stage. Appliqué motifs in yellow, green, pink and red silk are added between the resist-dyed sections – a strip of ribbon provides a splash of colour, while small triangles of silk adorn the corners of squares. A sewing machine is used for the ribbons, but the triangles are sewn on by hand. The fabric used for the appliqué designs is thin enough to allow very tight pleats. To finish the garment, the light-coloured decorative panels and the plain indigo sections are stiffened with rice starch, calendered, pleated and finally sewn together to form the skirt.

Opposite:
Pleated skirt. Plain indigo and cotton panels decorated with resist-dyed motifs. Silk pieces and synthetic ribbon. H. 52 cm, full width 520 cm. Green Miao people. Guizhou, China. Catherine Legrand Collection.

Above:
Green Miao women buying goods at the market in Pingyong, Guizhou, China.

CHILD'S JACKET AND BIB

Chinese textiles are adorned with a wide variety of symbolic motifs. These are often embroidered, but some are created using reverse appliqué, as seen on the jacket and bib shown here. They are often combined with standard appliqué and embroidery.

Baby carriers, bibs and children's hats and jackets are embellished with an array of designs: birds sent as messengers from the gods, flowers symbolizing abundance, butterflies (a favourite Miao symbol), star-shaped sweetgum leaves, dragons and fish, stars and spirals. The spirals evoke swirling water and symbolize the migration of the Miao people from the Huang He (Yellow River) to the Qing-shui-jiang River in Guizhou. They also represent the curved fronds of fiddlehead ferns, a common vegetable in Miao cuisine.

The bib is embellished with eight spirals and fastens over the baby's right shoulder. It is made from three layers of fabric: delicate red cotton, a lining of indigo-dyed hemp and – between these two – indigo-dyed cotton. To create a symmetrical design, the maker folded the red fabric into four, then used a

pair of scissors to cut the spiral motif into all four layers at the same time. She then unfolded the material and tacked it onto the indigo cotton base fabric. Next, using the point of her needle, she separated the fabric on either side of the cuts and turned the edges with small stitches, allowing the indigo layer underneath to show through. This is exactly the same technique as the one used by the Guna people, thousands of miles away in Panama (see p. 82). The bib is lined, with a hole for the baby's neck and a split over the shoulder, and the edges are finished with indigo binding. Two small white appliqué motifs have been added to the front.

The jacket shown opposite has forty-eight stars on the back and just as many on the front. It is a little faded from wear but still striking. As on the bib, these motifs have been created using reverse appliqué. There are three layers of fabric: a thick backing, an outer layer of fine cotton from which the star shapes have been cut, and a beige layer between the two. The centres of the stars are outlined with beige embroidery stitching. Some of the stars are edged with red braid, while others have a red circle appliquéd in the centre, hiding the fabric underneath. The jacket is made from a simple rectangle of fabric, folded over at the shoulders, with a split in the front and a piece cut away to form the neckhole. The sleeves were then attached to the central piece and the entire garment has been lined.

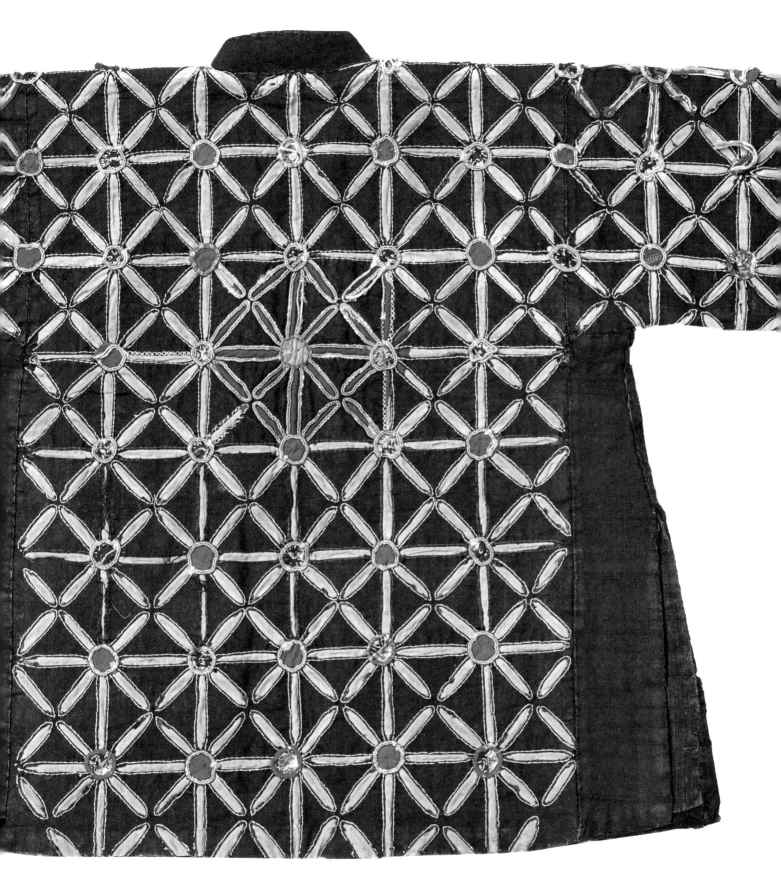

Opposite:
Bib. Cotton with reverse
appliqué motifs. Ties on the
right shoulder. 33 × 33 cm.
Guizhou, China. Liliane and
Armel Chichery Collection.

Above:
Child's jacket (rear). Cotton.
Reverse appliqué motifs.
H. 35 cm, w. 46 cm, arm span
68 cm. Guizhou, China. Liliane
and Armel Chichery Collection.

Jacket. Cotton, silk felt, silk thread. Cotton lining. H. 57 cm, arm span 141 cm. Miao people, Danzhai. Guizhou, China, early 20th century. Marie-Paule Raibaud Collection.

caterpillars reach maturity, they are deliberately not given any branches on which to spin their cocoons. Instead they are placed on a smooth board, which they cross again and again over the course of many days, leaving a trail of silk in all directions, until they die. These threads of silk interweave to form a fabric that resembles felt. This only takes place in springtime, around the month of May. The women who oversee the process must watch the silkworms constantly for four days, feeding them and cleaning up their droppings as they go. The finished silk felt is dyed, then cut into small pieces with the edges left raw, and used to make embellishments for clothes. In the neighbouring village of Zhouxi and in Shiqing, silk felt appliqué is traditionally used to embellish plastrons.

The woman's jacket shown here is a style that dates back to the early 20th century. It is a simple but elegant design, decorated with pink and black triangles of silk felt appliquéd onto an indigo fabric. It is rare to see such decorative restraint, especially in comparison with the elaborate styles currently made in the same region. The small right-angled triangles are carefully cut out, with unturned edges, then appliquéd onto the base fabric using backstitch in pink silk thread. The front and back of the jacket are both covered with bands of alternating black and pink triangles. Along the bottom edge of the jacket are three rows of stripes made from thin bands of black and pink appliqué, creating an effect somewhat similar to the ribbed hem of a sweater. The embellishment on the sleeves uses grey triangles instead of black. The only areas not covered by triangles are two bands of spiral resist-dyed motifs and two bands of plain indigo fabric, both on the sleeves.

MIAO JACKET FROM DANZHAI

The terraced rice fields of Gaoyao are a spectacular sight, and amply justify a visit to the region of Danzhai, formerly known as Bazhai, which lies between Kaili and Rongjiang, in Qiandongnan prefecture. Most people living in Danzhai are from the Miao ethnic group. In some villages, women still practise the complex art of making silk felt (*ghang-ah ao*).

The process of making silk felt is explained in detail by Marie-Claire Quiquemelle in her article 'Tissus et broderies miao de la province de Guizhou' (2004). Silkworm farms must be kept at a constant temperature; once the

YI SHAMAN'S TUNIC

The Yi people, also called the Nuosu, are a large ethnic group spread across many provinces in western and southwestern China. In the countryside of Yunnan and Sichuan provinces, the Yi community comes together every year to celebrate the Torch Festival, where they process around houses and fields carrying flaming torches, in order to ward off disease and insects.

The Yi people traditionally practise ancestor worship and their animist beliefs are combined with teachings from Buddhism and Taoism. Their rituals are performed by a shaman, called a *bino* or *binaw*, who is said to possess powers of divination, exorcism and healing. Shamans are highly respected by their communities as guardians of their ancient traditions. They wear special costumes to officiate at births, marriages and funerals. The garment shown here, made from cotton twill and decorated with a chequered pattern, is a narrow tunic with no fastenings; the square collar allows it to be slipped over the wearer's head. The sleeves, with added insets to form underarm gussets, are made from fabric with resist-dyed motifs. The front and back are covered with a patchwork design made up of almost 800 right-angled triangles sewn together in blocks of eight and appliquéd on. The range of subtle blues, beiges and pinks, probably created using plant-based dyes, give the piece a delicate beauty.

Silk farming and the cultivation of mulberry trees have been practised in China since time immemorial. There are many different ethnic groups that breed silkworms and use the harvested silk to make clothes. The silk can be turned into felt, by following the process described on page 199, or woven, as is the case for this shaman's tunic.

The fertilized eggs of the *Bombyx mori* moth hatch into caterpillars. Over the course of their lives, which lasts thirty-five to forty days, the silkworms moult four times. Placed in trays or on racks, they grow quickly, reaching almost 8 cm in length. They are fed exclusively on mulberry leaves (*Morus alba*). After their final moult, they stop eating and their bodies turn slightly yellow, the colour of raw silk. At this point, they are placed on a branch, which they attach themselves to by secreting threads. They then begin to weave their cocoon, moving in a figure of eight. The walls of the cocoon grow thicker and harder, and the silkworm disappears inside. Over the course of four or five days, its two silk glands secrete up to 1,500 metres of thread.

Once the cocoon is complete, the larva becomes a chrysalis, which will develop into a silk moth. A few adult moths are kept for breeding purposes, but most of the cocoons are harvested before their transformation is complete. The cocoons are submerged in hot water, killing the insect inside, and scraped out with a small brush that draws out the silk threads, a process known as 'degumming'. The spinner then joins multiple fibres into a single thread by hand. The thread is formed into a skein, washed and dyed.

Above and opposite (detail): Yi shaman's tunic. Indigo cotton twill covered with silk patchwork. Sleeves made of indigo cotton decorated with resist-dyed motifs. H. 130 cm, w. 43 cm, arm span 68 cm. Yunnan, China. Liliane and Armel Chichery Collection.

CHINA & FRANCE

YI SHAMAN'S TUNIC AND A CLERICAL ROBE DESIGNED BY MATISSE

Here is the tunic of a Yi shaman from Yunnan placed side by side with a liturgical robe designed by Henri Matisse, to be worn by the priest celebrating mass at the Chapel of the Rosary in Vence – a beautiful illustration of the global appeal of patchwork and appliqué.

Both garments are around 2 metres in width, and display a similar unfettered creativity in their plant-inspired motifs. In addition, both are designed to be worn by someone fulfilling a ceremonial or religious function, at the meeting point between the natural world and the spiritual realm; one to perform animist rituals and the other to celebrate the rites of the Catholic Church.

An unknown artisan cut out the garlands of flowers that adorn the Chinese tunic. They may be peonies, once the national flower of China, or may be meant to evoke the spiral shapes of fern fronds. These motifs appear on four panels of fabric in different shades of indigo. The overall design is a combination of curves and squares, large flowers and small checks, indigo and brown, the sky and the earth, two opposing but complementary forces.

The robes designed by Matisse were sewn by the Dominican nuns of Crépieux, near Lyons, craftswomen who specialized in making liturgical garments. Matisse described the designs pinned up on the walls of his studio as butterflies soaring through the heavens. The artist, whose father and grandfather were both weavers, had a passion for textiles and chose the fabric for these robes very carefully. He settled on silk poplin because it has a soft matt finish, the closest he could get to reproducing the feel of gouache on paper, which is what he used to paint the designs.

It is possible that these two pieces are contemporaneous; Matisse designed the robes for the chapel's opening in 1951.

A Yi shaman performing a ceremony and a Catholic priest celebrating mass: two men, separated by more than 2,000 km, both wear majestic garments with a spiritual dimension that far exceeds the modest sewing techniques used to create them.

Opposite above:
Chasuble designed by Henri Matisse for the Chapel of the Rosary, Vence. H. 129.5 cm, w. 196.9 cm. France, 1951. Museum of Modern Art, New York.

Right and opposite below:
Yi shaman's tunic. Chequered cotton, plain cotton dyed in two shades of indigo. Cut-out appliqué motifs. H. 122 cm, w. 240 cm. Yunnan, China, early 20th century. Claire and Pierre Ginioux Collection.

BIBLIOGRAPHY

ADLER Peter & BARNARD Nicholas, *African Majesty: The Textile Art of the Ashanti and Ewe*, London: Thames & Hudson, 1992

ADLER Peter & BARNARD Nicholas, *Asafo! African Flags of the Fante*, London: Thames & Hudson, 1992

African Costumes and Textiles From the Berbers to the Zulus: The Zaira and Marcel Mis Collection, Milan: 5 Continents, 2008

Autour du fil. L'encyclopédie des arts textiles, Paris: Éditions Fogtdal, 1988–91

BEAMISH Kim, *Tentmakers of Chareh El Khiamiah*, documentary film, 2012

BERENSON Kathryn, *Quilts of Provence: The Art and Craft of French Quiltmaking*, New York: Henry Holt & Company, 1996

BEYER Jinny, *Art and Technique of Creating Medallion Quilts*, McLean, VI: EPM Publications, 1982

BIEHN Michel, *En jupon piqué et robe d'indienne. Costumes provençaux*, Marseilles: Éditions Jeanne Laffitte, 1987

BISHOP Robert, *New Discoveries in American Quilts*, New York: E.P. Dutton, 1975

BOUDOT Éric, HENRY Lionel & RAIBAUD Marie-Paule, *Costumes traditionnels de la Chine du Sud-Ouest*, exhibition catalogue, Musée des Tissus, Lyons, *'L'Objet d'art'* no. 4, 2002

BOUILLOC Christine, MAURIÈRES Arnaud & SEYNHAEVE Marie-Bénédicte, *Tapis et textiles du Maroc à la Syrie*, Paris: Chêne, 2009

BOURZAT Catherine, *Tribal Textiles from Southwest China: Threads from Misty Lands*, Bangkok: River Books, 2016

BRACKMAN Barbara, *Clues in the Calico: A Guide to Identifying and Dating Antique Quilts*, Lafayette, CA: C&T Publishing, 2009

BROIN Charles-Édouard de, *Les Mille Bonheurs d'un chercheur de quilts*, Saint-Étienne-de-Montluc: Quiltmania, 2019

BROUILLET Isabel & GÉRIMONT Patricia, *Bleu noir. Teinturières d'indigo au pays dogon*, Saint-Maur: Éditions Sépia, 2021

BRUNA Denis & DEMEY Chloé (eds.), *Histoire des modes et du vêtement. Du Moyen Âge au XXIe siècle*, Paris: Textuel, 2018

BRUNNER Kathleen, DUMAS Ann et al., *Matisse, His Art and His Textiles: The Fabric of Dreams*, London: Royal Academy of Arts, 2004

BUNN Stephanie, *Nomadic Felts*, London: British Museum Press, 2011

CALLAÑAUPA ALVAREZ Nilda & FRANQUEMONT Christine, *Faces of Tradition: Weaving Elders of the Andes*, Loveland, CO: Thrums, 2013

CELANT Germano, *Louise Bourgeois: The Fabric Works*, Milan: Skira, 2010

CEVOLI Daria (ed.), *Esthétiques de l'Amour. Sibérie extrême-orientale*, Paris: Flammarion/Musée du Quai Branly, 2015

COLLINS Linda, *Treasures from the Barn*, Saint-Étienne-de-Montluc: Quiltmania, 2016

CORNU Georgette & KALLAB Oussama, 'Une robe de fillette libanaise d'époque mamelouke', in *Archéologie islamique*, no. 5, 1995

CORRIGAN Gina, *Miao Textiles from China*, London: British Museum Press, 2001

COUSIN Françoise, *Chemins de couleurs. Teintures et motifs du monde*, Paris: Musée du Quai Branly, 2008

De fil et d'argent. Mémoire des Miao de Chine, Milan: 5 Continents; Paris: Musée des Arts Asiatiques, 2004

DUMAS Ly, *Ndop: Étoffes des cours royales et sociétés secrètes du Cameroun*, Montreuil: Gourcuff Gradenigo, 2020

EDWARDS Eiluned, *Textiles and Dress of Gujarat*, Middletown, NJ: Grantha, 2011

FALGAYRETTES-LEVEAU Christiane (ed.), *Mascarades et carnavals*, Paris: Musée Dapper, 2011

FAUQUE Claude, *Le Patchwork ou La désobéissance*, Paris: Syros-Alternatives, 1993

FISHER Nora, FRATER Judy et al., *Mud, Mirror and Thread: Folk Traditions of Rural India*, Santa Fe: Museum of New Mexico Press, 1993

FRATER Judy, *Threads of Identity: Embroidery and Adornment of the Nomadic Rabaris*, Middletown, NJ: Grantha, 1995

GABERT Sylvette & GIRAUD Marie-Christine, *Le Costume comtadin*, Brantes: Éditions du Toulourenc, 2009

GARDI Bernhard, *Le Boubou, c'est chic*, Paris: Musée des Arts d'Afrique et d'Océanie; Basel: Museum der Kulturen Basel, 2000

GERO Annette, *Wartime Quilts: Appliqués and Geometric Masterpieces from Military Fabrics*, Roseville, Australia: The Beagle Press, 2015

GILLOW John & BARNARD Nicholas, *Indian Textiles*, London: Thames & Hudson, 2014

GILLOW John, *Textiles of the Islamic World*, London: Thames & Hudson, 2013

GRENOT-WANG Françoise, *Chine du Sud: La Mosaïque des minorités*, Paris: Les Indes Savantes, 2005

GROSFILLEY Anne, *Fibres africaines. Patrimoine et savoir-faire textiles d'un continent*, Milan: Silvana Editoriale; Jouy-en-Josas: Musée de la Toile de Jouy, 2020

GUNN Virginia, *Yo-yo or Bed of Roses Quilts: Nineteenth-Century Origins*, Lincoln, NE: American Quilt Study Group, 1987

HARVEY Janet, *Traditional Textiles of Central Asia*, London: Thames & Hudson, 2005

HEMMET Christine, *Montagnards des pays d'Indochine dans les collections du musée de l'Homme*, Paris: Éditions Sépia, 1995

HOLSTEIN Jonathan & FINLAY John, *Kentucky Quilts 1800–1900*, New York: Pantheon Books, 1983

HOLSTEIN Jonathan, *The Pieced Quilt: An American Design Tradition*, Greenwich, CT: Galahad Books, 1973

HUBERT Jean-François (ed.), *Le Viêt Nam des royaumes*, Paris: Cercle d'Art, 1995

INNES Miranda, *Rags to Rainbows: Traditional Quilting, Patchwork and Appliqué from Around the World*, London: Collins & Brown, 1992

JANNIÈRE Janine, *Mosaïques d'étoffes. À la recherche de l'hexagone*, exhibition catalogue, Château de Martainville; Rouen: Conseil Général de Seine-Maritime, 2003

JONES Jen, *Welsh Quilts*, Saint-Étienne-de-Montluc: Quiltmania, 2005

KALTER Johannes & PAVALOI Margareta, *Uzbekistan: Heirs to the Silk Road*, London: Thames & Hudson, 1997

KHANDELWAL Geeta, *Godharis of Maharashtra, Western India*, Saint-Étienne-de-Montluc: Quiltmania, 2013

Kimonos d'enfants (1860–1930), collection de Kazuko Nakano, exhibition catalogue, Paris: Bibliothèque Forney/Amitiés Tissées, 2012

KIRACOFE Roderick, *The American Quilt: A History of Cloth and Comfort, 1750–1950*, New York: Clarkson Potter, 2004

KOIDE Yukiko & TSUZUKI Kyoichi, *Boro: Rags and Tatters from the Far North of Japan*, Tokyo: Aspect Corp., 2009

KWON Charlotte & McLAUGHLIN Tim, *Textiles of the Banjara*, London: Thames & Hudson, 2016

LAMB Venice & Alastair, *Au Cameroun, Weaving – Tissage*, Douala, Cameroon: Elf Serepca, 1981

LÉGERET Jacques & Catherine, *Quilts amish*, Geneva: Labor et Fides, 2001

LÉGERET Jacques, *L'Énigme amish. Vivre au XXIe siècle comme au XVIIe*, Geneva: Labor et Fides, 2000

LÉGERET Jacques, *Les Amish et leurs quilts*, Saint-Remy-de-Provence: Édisud; Clermont-Ferrand: Musée du Tapis, 2006

LÉGERET Jacques, *Quilts amish et mennonites*, exhibition catalogue, Château de Goulaine; Saint-Étienne-de-Montluc: Quiltmania, 1998

LE GOAZIOU Marie, *Patchwork. Contre-Cultures*, Paris: Éditions Courtes et Longues, 2019

LEGRAND Catherine & GRATACAP Elisabeth, *À La Bonne Renommée. 136 saisons*, Paris: Somogy Éditions d'Art, 2011

LEGRAND Catherine, *Carnet d'inspirations textiles*, Paris: Éditions de La Martinière, 2008

LEGRAND Catherine, *De la tête aux pieds*, Paris: Éditions de La Martinière, 2017

LEGRAND Catherine, *Indigo: The Colour that Changed the World*, London: Thames & Hudson, 2012

LEGRAND Catherine, *Textiles: A World Tour*, London: Thames & Hudson, 2008

LEWIS Paul & Elaine, *Peoples of the Golden Triangle: Six Tribes in Thailand*, London: Thames & Hudson, 1984

LURY Jane, *Meanderings of a Quilt Collector*, Saint-Étienne-de-Montluc: Quiltmania, 2016

MABÉLÉ Claude, *Syrie. Les artisans du textile*, Paris: Magellan & Cie, 2012

MACKENZIE MOON Ryan, *African Apparel: Threaded Transformations Across the Twentieth Century*, New York: Scala; Ithaca, NY: Cornell Museum Collection, 2020

McMORRIS Penny, *Crazy Quilts*, New York: E.P. Dutton, 1984

MELLER Susan, *Silk and Cotton: Textiles From the Central Asia That Was*, New York: Abrams, 2013

Mémoire de soie: Costumes et parures de Palestine et de Jordanie, catalogue of the Widad Kamel Kawar collection, Paris: Institut du Monde Arabe/EDIFRA, 1988

MOONEN An, *A History of Dutch Quilts*, Utrecht: Van Gruting, 2010

MURRAY Thomas, *Textiles of Japan*, Munich: Prestel, 2018

NELSON Cyril I. & HOUCK Carter, *The Quilt Engagement Calendar Treasury*, New York: E.P. Dutton, 1982

ORMSBY STODDARD Patricia, *Ralli Quilts: Traditional Textiles from Pakistan and India*, Atglen, PA: Shiffer Publishing, 2003

PELLMAN Rachel & Kenneth, *Amish Crib Quilts*, Intercourse, PA: Good Books, 1985

PELLMAN Rachel & Kenneth, *The World of Amish Quilts*, Intercourse, PA: Good Books, 1984

PERRIER Michel, *Mosaïque d'étoffes*, Saint-Étienne-de-Montluc: Quiltmania, 2001

PERRIN Michel, *Magnificent Molas: The Art of the Kuna Indians*, Paris: Flammarion, 1999

PICTON John & MACK John, *African Textiles*, London: British Museum Press, 1979

POTTINGER David, *Quilts from the Indiana Amish*, New York: E.P. Dutton, 1983

POURRET Jess G., *The Yao: The Mien and Mun Yao in China, Vietnam, Laos and Thailand*, Chicago: Art Media Resources, 2002

PRICHARD Sue, *Quilts 1700–2010. Hidden Histories, Untold Stories*, London: V&A Publishing, 2010

Quilt Art: L'art du patchwork, exhibition catalogue, Paris: Mona Bismarck American Center, 2013

QUIQUEMELLE Marie-Claire, 'Tissus et broderies miao de la province du Guizhou en Chine', in *Arts asiatiques*, no. 59, 2004

RAIBAUD Marie-Paule, *Femmes d'une autre Chine*, Béziers: Éditions du Mont, 2004

SAFFORD Carleton L. & BISHOP Robert, *America's Quilts and Coverlets*, New York: E.P. Dutton, 1972

SIKE Yvonne de, *Fiers Magyars. Splendeurs des manteaux hongrois*, Budapest: Museum of Ethnography; Paris: Musée de l'Homme, 2001

SUH Jae-sik, *Korean Patterns*, Carlsbad, CA: Hollym, 2007

SULEMAN Fahmida, *The Fabric of Life: Textiles of the Middle East and Central Asia*, London: Thames & Hudson, 2017

SUMBERG Bobbie, *Textiles: Collection of the Museum of International Folk Art*, Layton, UT: Gibbs Smith, 2010

Syrie. Signes d'étoffe, Paris: Maison des Cultures du Monde/ACL Éditions, 1989

TAKEDA Sharon Sadako & ROBERTS Luke S., *Japanese Fishermen's Coats from Awaji Island*, Los Angeles: UCLA Fowler Museum of Cultural History, 2001

TORIMARU Tomoko & Sadae, *Imprints on Cloth: 18 Years of Field Research among the Miao People of Guizhou, China*, Fukuoka: Nishinippon Newspaper Co., 2004

TORIMARU Tomoko, *One Needle, One Thread: Miao (Hmong) Embroidery and Fabric Piecework from Guizhou, China*, Honolulu: University of Hawaii Art Gallery, 2008

VADIM Vanessa & ARNETT Matthew, *The Quilts of Gee's Bend*, DVD, Tinwood Media, 2006

Vietnam Museum of Ethnology, Hanoi: Vietnam Museum of Ethnology, 1997

WEARDEN Jennifer & BAKER Patricia L., *Iranian Textiles*, London: V&A Publishing, 2010

WEIR Shelagh, *Embroidery from Palestine*, London: British Museum Press, 2006

WETTRE Åsa, *Old Swedish Quilts*, Fort Collins, CO: Interweave Press, 1995

YOUNG-HEE Lee, *L'Étoffe des rêves*, Paris: Musée National des Arts Asiatiques Guimet/Éditions de La Martinière, 2019

ZACEK BASSETT Lynne (ed.), *Massachusetts Quilts: Our Common Wealth*, Lebanon, NH: University Press of New England, 2009.

ACKNOWLEGMENTS

I dedicate this book to my accomplice in patchwork, Elisabeth Gratacap.

My deepest thanks to everyone who contributed to this book: to the many friends who entrusted their works to me in order to provide illustrations, and to the dealers, collectors and institutions who made their knowledge and their photographs available to me.

My special thanks go to Géraldine Chouard-Véron, professor of American studies specializing in visual culture at the Université Paris-Dauphine and curator of patchwork exhibitions, for her enlightening contribution to the chapter on the USA.

I would also like to thank the team at Éditions de La Martinière, editors Aude Mantoux, Anne-Laure Cognet and Eva Levêque, Marko Dapic for his photography, Séverine Morizet for the layout design and Laurence Alvado, picture researcher and proofreader.

Thanks also to Yves Halifa whose support has never failed me.

Catherine Legrand
www.in-di-go.fr

MANY THANKS TO:

Maryse Allard

Monique Alphand

Lena Bibring

Philippe Boudin
Galerie Mingei, Japanese Arts, Paris
www.mingei-arts-gallery.com

Christine Bouilloc, Charlotte Croissant, Thibault Jamois & Emilie Robert
Musée Bargoin, Clermont-Ferrand

Charles-Édouard de Broin
www.patchwork-quilts-americains.com

Liliane & Armel Chichery

Tuulikki Chompré

Duncan Clarke
Adire African Textiles Gallery, London
www.adireafricantextiles.com

Anna Dolanyi

Marguerite Faust

Sylvette Gabert & Régine Feret
Conservatoire du Costume Comtadin,
Pernes-les-Fontaines
www.costumescomtadin.com

Patricia Gérimont
https://fr-fr.facebook.com/textilesmali

Claire & Pierre Ginioux
Arts Premiers & Bijoux Sorciers
www.ginioux-tribal.fr

Viktoria Holmqvist
Textilmuseet, Borås

Marie-Bénédicte Kermorgant

Jacques & Catherine Légeret
www.quiltsamish.com

Marina Lussato Fedier
Institut Bruno Lussato, Brussels
www.brunolussatoinstitute.be

Claude Mabélé

Susan Meller

Patrick & Ondine Mestdagh
Galerie Patrick & Ondine Mestdagh, Brussels
www.galeriemestdagh.com

Bruno Mignot
Galerie Bruno Mignot, La Wantzenau
www.bruno-mignot.com

An Moonen

Kazuko Nakano

Dominique Niorthe

Karin Nordberg

Michel Perrier

Marie-Paule Raibaud

Edith Raymond

Nicole Roca

Léa Stansal
www.leastansal.com

Stina Svantesson
Västergötlands Museum, Skara

Yves Venot & Daniel Cendron

Shukuko Voss-Tabe
Amitiés Tissées
www.amitiestissees.com

Wahid Wazir
www.instagram.com/wahid_wazir

Åsa Wettre

Christopher Wilson-Tate
Antique Textiles Company, London
www.antiquetextilescompany.co.uk

Amit Zadok

PICTURE CREDITS

ABOUT THE AUTHOR

Catherine Legrand is a designer and co-founder of the brand À La Bonne Renommée. Over the course of her travels, she has become a passionate collector of textiles, costumes, costume jewelry and accessories. She was the curator of the exhibition 'Indigo', which toured various museums in France and abroad. Her other books include *Textiles: A World Tour* and *Indigo: The Colour That Changed the World*, both published by Thames & Hudson.

On the cover:
Detail of an African American quilt (see p. 74).
Charles-Édouard de Broin Collection.

Text translated from the French *Patchworks. Une mosaïque du monde*
by Bethany Wright and Ruth Taylor

First published in the United Kingdom in 2022 by
Thames & Hudson Ltd, 181A High Holborn, London WC1V 7QX

First published in the United States of America in 2023 by
Thames & Hudson Inc., 500 Fifth Avenue, New York, New York 10110

Original edition © 2022 Éditions de La Martinière,
a trademark of EDLM, 57 rue Gaston Tessier, 75019 Paris.
This edition © 2022 Thames & Hudson Ltd, London

British Library Cataloguing-in-Publication Data.
A catalogue record for this book is available from the British Library

Library of Congress Control Number 2022938462

ISBN 978-0-500-02581-9

Printed in Portugal

Be the first to know about our new releases,
exclusive content and author events by visiting
thamesandhudson.com
thamesandhudsonusa.com
thamesandhudson.com.au